本教材获教育部中外语言交流合作中心项目资助项目号 21YH052CX5

Basic Legal Chinese

基础法律汉语（下册）

主 编 — 许 兰　马琳琳

撰稿人 — 马琳琳　刘 芳

张 翀　朱远勃

中国政法大学出版社

2025·北京

图书在版编目（CIP）数据

基础法律汉语. 下册 / 许兰，马琳琳主编. -- 北京 ：中国政法大学出版社，2025. 7. -- ISBN 978-7-5764-2200-9

Ⅰ. H195.4

中国国家版本馆 CIP 数据核字第 2025L3K626 号

书　　名	基础法律汉语（下册）JI CHU FA LÜ HAN YU　（ XIA CE ）	
出 版 者	中国政法大学出版社	
地　　址	北京市海淀区西土城路25号	
邮　　箱	fadapress@163.com	
网　　址	http://www.cuplpress.com (网络实名：中国政法大学出版社)	
电　　话	010-58908435(第一编辑部) 58908334(邮购部)	
承　　印	北京中科印刷有限公司	
开　　本	720mm×960mm　1/16	
印　　张	14	
字　　数	207千字	
版　　次	2025年7月第1版	
印　　次	2025年7月第1次印刷	
定　　价	69.00元	

作者简介

许　兰　女，中国政法大学教授。曾任国际合作与交流处处长，中国政法大学国际教育学院院长。现任中国驻泰国大使馆教育参赞。

马琳琳　女，中国政法大学国际教育学院教师。学术研究领域：语言学及应用语言学、中国法律史、国际中文教育等。

刘　芳　女，中国政法大学国际教育学院教师。学术研究领域：第二语言习得、国际中文教育等。

张　翀　女，中国政法大学人权研究院副编审、智库内参编辑部主任。主要研究领域：人权理论、法哲学和法律思想史。

朱远勋　女，中国政法大学国际教育学院教师。学术研究领域：教育学、国际中文教育等。

前　言

　　中国法律文明源远流长。从先秦时期到今天，始终在不断进步。而伴随中国历史的发展脉络，中国古代法律传统和法律文化逐渐形成并演进，与中华法系共融共生，不仅是中国历史的一部分，更是中华文明的一部分。

　　中国古代法律文化的核心是"礼法"，并自汉代开始，逐渐与儒家思想相融合。随着历史阶段的演变，各个朝代在法律建设上既有继承又有创新，形成了丰富的具有中国特色的法律传统。

适用对象

　　本教材适用于具有中文中级以上水平的国际学生，也可以作为中文以及中国文化学习者的参考资料。

编写理念

　　本教材以中国法律史和法律文化发展的脉络为主线，可使学习者在中国古代法律的发展历程与法文化中学习中文。因此，教材不仅仅关注中国法律史与法律文化本身，更从中文学习的角度出发，帮助学习者了解中文深层的文化底色。

编写原则

　　本教材在编写过程中，力求做到以下几点：首先，注重中国法律发展史的脉络；其次，强调法律发展过程中与社会文化的互动；最后，通过法文化展现中文的语言特色。

教材结构

本教材分为上下两册，每册 12 课，共 24 课。其中，上册从中国法律的起源到唐朝；下册从宋朝到清朝末年。每课教学课时建议为 3—4 课时。本册为教材的上册。每课主要安排如下：

【课前准备】与本课相关的中国历史发展简介

【导　　读】与本课课文相关的中国法律史内容

【课　　文】需要重点了解的中国法律史、法文化相关内容，及相关生词

【重点汉字】本课重点学习的法文化高频字

【文化知识】与本课所涉历史朝代相关的中国历史文化知识

【法治文物】与中国法文化相关的法治文物

【经典阅读】与本课所涉历史朝代相关的古代典籍

主要特色

本教材最大的特色是：以中国法律制度史为纲，以系统性的法律文化知识为桥梁，进行中文学习，特别在每一课列出中国法文化的高频字。其中，高频字的选取以《说文解字》为基础、以《唐律疏议》为参考、根据法律词语语域界定的标准，并结合现代法学概念和出现的频率。教材同时配有沉浸式动画版，学习者可以扫描后文二维码进入学习。

撰写分工

许　兰　大纲编制及全书定稿

马琳琳　第一课、第二课、第三课、第四课，全书统稿及校改

刘　芳　第五课、第六课

张　翀　第七课、第八课、第九课

朱远勍　第十课、第十一课、第十二课

特别致谢

中国政法大学法律史学研究院 朱勇教授

中国政法大学法律古籍整理研究所 李雪梅教授

我们希望，通过本教材，学习者能够在掌握中国古代法律基本知识的基础上，形成对中国法律文化的全面认识，并对中文有更深入的了解；进而为理解和参与现代法治建设提供历史借鉴和文化滋养。

编　者

2025 年 3 月

本教材所用语法术语及缩略语形式参照表

Grammar Terms in Chinese	Grammar Terms in English	Abbreviations
名词	noun	*n.*
动词	verb	*v.*
形容词	adjective	*adj.*
成语	idiom	*idm.*
短语	phrase	*phr.*
专有名词	proper noun	*proper n.*

本教材沉浸式动画下载地址

目　录

CONTENTS

第一课

宋朝时期的法律（一）

（课）前准备

图 1-1 北宋·《千里江山图》(王希孟)

公元 960 年，后周禁军将领赵匡胤发动"陈桥兵变"夺取政权，建立宋朝，定都东京（今河南省开封市），史称北宋。1127 年，金兵南侵，宋王朝被迫南迁，后定都临安（今浙江省杭州市），史称南宋；直至 1279 年，南宋为元朝所灭。两宋在法制建设上基本承袭唐朝制度，又根据当时的经济政治形势新的发展，多所变革，最终形成自己的特色，成就了中国法律史上新的辉煌。[1]

In AD 960, Zhao Kuangyin, a military leader of the Later Zhou Dynasty, launched "The Mutiny of Chenqiao Posthouse" and seized power, establishing the Song Dynasty with its capital at Dongjing (present-day Kaifeng, Henan), known historically as the Northern Song Dynasty. In 1127, the Jin forces invaded from the north, forcing the Song Dynasty to relocate its capital to Lin'an (present-day Hangzhou, Zhejiang), marking the beginning of the Southern Song Dynasty. The Southern Song Dynasty was ultimately conquered by the Yuan Dynasty in 1279. Both the Northern and Southern Song Dynasties largely inherited the legal system of the Tang Dynasty, but made

---

〔1〕 参见朱勇主编：《中国法律史》，中国政法大学出版社 2021 年版，第 196 页。

numerous reforms in response to the changing economic and political situations of the time, thus creating distinctive features and achieving a new era of brilliance in the history of Chinese law.

 生词表

序号	生词	词性	汉语拼音	英文解释
1	禁军	*n.*	jìn jūn	imperial guards
2	陈桥兵变	*proper n.*	Chén qiáo Bīng biàn	the mutiny incident in which Zhao Kuangyin overthrew the Later Zhou Dynasty and established the Song Dynasty
3	夺取	*v.*	duó qǔ	seize, capture
4	定都	*v.*	dìng dū	establish the capital
5	被迫	*v.*	bèi pò	be forced, be compelled
6	迁	*v.*	qiān	move, migrate
7	承袭	*v.*	chéng xí	inherit, adopt

 读

　　北宋政权建立后，面临削弱割据势力、巩固国家统一、恢复社会安定和促进经济发展等一系列问题。为此，宋太祖曾与赵普等人反复探讨。赵普针对地方提出**"稍夺其权，制其钱谷，收其精兵"**（《续资治通鉴长编》）的对策，将兵权、财权、司法权全部集中到中央，进而"强干弱枝"，做到政出于一、权归于上，使中央和地方**"上下相维，轻重相制，如身之使臂，臂之使指"**（《范太史集》）。然而，集权中央并没有消除宋朝日趋严重的社会问题，冗官冗员、积贫积弱，内部矛盾的激化与外部少数民族政权的侵扰，促使北宋政权不断地寻求解决办法。[1]

―――――――――――

〔1〕 参见朱勇主编：《中国法律史》，中国政法大学出版社 2021 年版，第 196 页。

宋仁宗庆历年间和宋神宗熙宁年间有两次重要的变法改革。

北宋仁宗的"庆历新政"是一场旨在挽救宋朝危机、富国强兵的政治改革，由范仲淹主导。这场改革从1043年开始，至1045年即因范仲淹、韩琦、富弼、欧阳修等人被排挤出朝廷而告终。"庆历新政"涉及政治、经济、军事、社会及文化等多个领域，其核心是整顿吏治、减少冗官和冗兵、解决财政冗费等问题。改革期间，通过严格的考核机制淘汰了一大批无能或腐败的官员，而有能力的实干官员则被提拔至关键职位，显著提升了行政效率和财政状况；漕运等关键经济指标也得到改善，政局初见回暖。然而，新政实施后，恩荫减少，磨勘严密，指责范仲淹是"朋党"的议论再度兴起，最终范仲淹等人相继被罢黜，各项改革措施也被废除，庆历新政以失败告终。新政不仅未能

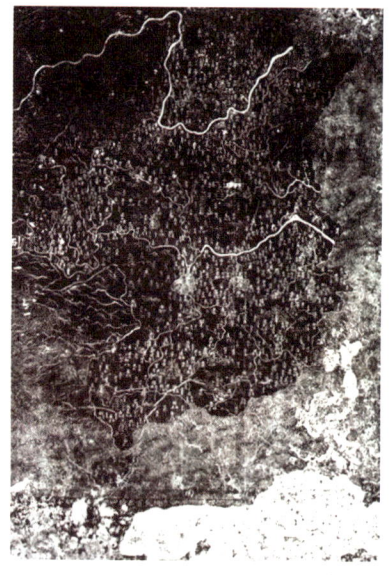

图 1-2　宋·《九域守令图》[1]

---

〔1〕 转引自《法制文物日历｜四月七日·宋·九域守令图》，载"中国政法大学法律古籍整理研究所"公众号2021年4月7日，https://mp.weixin.qq.com/s/Whxk5VGLAmRaTivzp9sIzw，最后访问日期：2025年5月30日。

根本解决政治和社会问题，其失败反而使得土地兼并更加严重，财政负担进一步加重，社会矛盾和民族矛盾更为尖锐。这成为后来宋神宗时期王安石变法的直接动因。

　　宋神宗时期的"王安石变法"，于 1069 年开始，至 1085 年宋神宗去世时结束，也称"熙宁变法"或"熙丰变法"。该变法同样以富国强兵、发展生产为目的，主要集中在财政和整顿军队上，是继"王莽改制"之后中国古代史上又一次规模巨大的政治变革。尽管变法增加了政府的财政收入，并推进了军队建设，但执行中出现的问题导致了民众负担加重，而新旧党派的争斗又使政局更为复杂。王安石本人两次因朝内压力而辞去相位，但在神宗的支持下新法仍基本推行。神宗去世后，宣仁太后和司马光的上台导致新法几乎被全面废除。

 生词表

序号	生词	词性	汉语拼音	英文解释
1	庆历新政	*proper n.*	Qìng lì Xīn zhèng	a political reform implemented during the Qingli period of the Northern Song Dynasty
2	挽救	*v.*	wǎn jiù	save，rescue
3	富国强兵	*idm.*	fù guó qiáng bīng	enrich the country and strengthen the military
4	排挤	*v.*	pái jǐ	squeeze out
5	整顿	*v.*	zhěng dùn	rectify，reorganize
6	冗官	*n.*	rǒng guān	redundant officials
7	冗兵	*n.*	rǒng bīng	redundant soldiers
8	冗费	*n.*	rǒng fèi	redundant expenses
9	淘汰	*v.*	táo tài	eliminate
10	漕运	*v.*	cáo yùn	grain transport by water
11	兼并	*v.*	jiān bìng	annex，merge

续表

序号	生词	词性	汉语拼音	英文解释
12	熙宁变法	*proper n.*	Xī níng Biàn fǎ	a reform implemented during the Xining period of the Northern Song Dynasty
13	新旧	*phr.*	xīn jiù	new and old
14	党派	*n.*	dǎng pài	political faction，party
15	宣仁太后	*proper n.*	Xuān rén Tài hòu	Empress Dowager Xuanren，the mother of Emperor Shenzong of the Northern Song Dynasty
16	司马光	*proper n.*	Sī mǎ Guāng	a statesman in the Northern Song Dynasty

重 点汉字【诏】

　　诏，汉语二级字。本义是"告知、告诉"，后来特指帝王所发的文书命令，如诏书、诏令、诏谕等。先秦时期尚未出现"诏"字，直至秦朝正式将"诏"用于上告下的场合。如《说文解字》："诏，告也"；《礼记正义》："出入有诏于国"；蔡邕《独断》："诏书者"；《穆天子传》："以诏后世"；《史记》："于是上乃使使持节诏将军"。

图1-3 "诏"字篆刻（王琦 刻）

汉字拓展

序号	词汇	汉语拼音	英文解释	例句
1	诏书	zhào shū	imperial edict	皇帝发出诏书，宣布新的税收政策。
2	奉诏	fèng zhào	receive an imperial command	大臣奉诏前往边境地区检查防御工事。
3	诏令	zhào lìng	imperial order	皇帝发布诏令，全国征兵。
4	诏命	zhào mìng	imperial command	他被赐予诏命，授予边防总督的职务。
5	诏狱	zhào yù	prison by imperial command	诏狱是中国古代奉皇帝命令拘捕犯人的监狱。
6	诏告	zhào gào	proclaim of the emperor	国王诏告天下，即将举行加冕仪式。
7	诏赦	zhào shè	imperial amnesty	新皇登基之际，发布诏赦，释放了许多犯人。

文 化知识【宋词】

　　宋词是中国宋代盛行的一种重要文学体裁，是在唐代诗歌的基础上发展起来的一种诗乐形式。它融合了文学与音乐的双重特质，既有诗的精练语言，又借助曲调的情感表现力，被誉为宋代文学的瑰宝。宋词和唐诗并称"唐诗宋词"，是中国文学史上的两颗明珠。

　　宋词，简称"词"，是配合乐曲演唱的歌词，起源于隋唐时期，在宋代达到了鼎盛。词的长短不一，被称为"长短句"，词调丰富多样，每首词有固定的格律和韵律。宋词通常分为小令、中调和长调，以不同篇幅表达多种多样的情感和意境。宋词的语言优美而富有韵律，讲究情景交融，强调以词表达丰富的情感和细腻的心理。它通过特定的词牌（如《蝶恋花》《水调歌头》）来创作，每个词牌有独特的韵律和结构，表现的主题也各不相同。

图1-4　宋·《文会图》(赵佶等)

　　宋词的主要流派分为婉约派和豪放派两大类。婉约派主要盛行于北宋前期，词风细腻、柔美，侧重抒发个人情感，尤其擅长表现男女爱情、离愁别绪等细腻感情。代表词人包括柳永、晏殊、欧阳修和李清照等。豪放派兴起于北宋中后期，一般认为由苏轼开创，强调词的思想深度和宏大情怀，以激昂、奔放的语言来表达胸怀大志或描绘壮丽景象。

　　苏轼是宋词豪放派的创始人之一，他将词从传统的小情小调中解放出来，将词的表现内容扩展到历史、哲理、山水等方面，形成了气势磅礴、充满哲理的豪放风格。其代表作《念奴娇·赤壁怀古》是豪放派词作品的典范，展示了苏轼对历史的深刻反思和旷达的人生态度。豪放派的另一个代表人物辛弃疾继承并发扬了苏轼的豪放风格，其词充满了爱国情怀和抗敌救国的壮志。《破阵子·为陈同甫赋壮词以寄之》是辛弃疾豪放词的代表，表现了他对英勇抗敌的渴望。

宋词作为宋代文学的精华，展现了当时文人的才情和对生活的独特理解，不仅在内容上表现了丰富的人生体验，还在形式上注重音律与语言的结合，对后世的文学创作产生了深远的影响，是中国古代文学的璀璨瑰宝。

法 治文物【《大宋东岳天齐仁圣帝碑》】

《大宋东岳天齐仁圣帝碑》又名《祥符碑》，螭首龟趺，高 820 厘米，宽 215 厘米，厚 60 厘米。额篆"大宋东岳天 / 齐仁圣帝碑"2 行 10 字。碑阳 34 行，满行 80 字，翰林学士晁迥撰文，翰林待诏、朝散大夫尹熙古行书并篆额。

碑文记录了自唐玄宗至宋真宗期间为泰山神累加封号的过程。唐开元十三年（725 年）封泰山神为"天齐王"，寓意与天相齐。宋真宗于大中祥符元年（1008 年）举行了规模空前的泰山封禅大典，告成之后下诏加号泰山为"仁圣天齐王"，并修饰庙宇；大中祥符四年（1011 年）晋泰山神号为"天齐仁圣帝"。泰山神由"王"而"帝"，地位至为尊崇。

碑阴刻有"五岳独宗"4 个榜书大字，系明万历二十四年（1596 年）巡抚张允济、巡按王立贤所题。巨碑上的榜书气度恢宏，彰显了泰山独一无二的崇高地位。

图 1-5 《大宋东岳天齐仁圣帝碑》碑阴[1]

---

〔1〕 参见《大宋东岳天齐仁圣帝碑》，载中国政法大学中华法制文明虚拟博物馆，https://flgj.cupl.edu.cn/info/1092/4064.html，最后访问日期：2025 年 2 月 27 日。

经 典阅读（宋词代表作范例）

《雨霖铃·寒蝉凄切》
（柳永）

寒蝉凄切，对长亭晚，骤雨初歇。都门帐饮无绪，留恋处，兰舟催发。执手相看泪眼，竟无语凝噎。念去去，千里烟波，暮霭沉沉楚天阔。

多情自古伤离别，更那堪，冷落清秋节！今宵酒醒何处？杨柳岸，晓风残月。此去经年，应是良辰好景虚设。便纵有千种风情，更与何人说？

 参考译文

秋蝉凄切地鸣叫，傍晚时分我们在长亭分别，大雨刚刚停下。都城外的帐中设宴饯行，心中却充满了离愁，没有心情欢饮。正在依依不舍的时候，船已经催促着要出发，我们手拉着手，眼泪蒙眬地对视，却哽咽得说不出话。想到这次分别，我将远行千里，烟波浩渺，暮霭沉沉，楚天广阔，一片茫然。

自古以来多情的人最难忍受离别，何况现在是冷清的秋天。今夜醒来后，我将在何处？只有杨柳岸边黎明时分的凄风和残月相伴。这一去长年相别，哪怕有美好的时光和风景，也只是如同虚设。即使心中有满腹的情意，又能向谁诉说？

Autumn cicadas cry mournfully. We part at the pavilion at dusk, as the rain has just ceased. We hold a farewell banquet in the tent outside the capital city, but our hearts are filled with melancholy, and we have no appetite for enjoying the feast. Just as we are reluctant to part with each other, the boat is already hurrying to set sail. We hold hands, gazing into tearful eyes, but words fail us as we choke with sobs. As I contemplate this separation and the long journey ahead, there will be thousands of miles of misty waves, the evening mist will hang heavy, and the vast expanse of the southern sky will seem so desolate.

Ever since ancient times, those who are passionate and affectionate find it the hardest to endure separation, especially during the bleak autumn season. Where will I wake up after tonight's drunkenness? I will be by the willow-covered riverbank, accompanied by the desolate morning breeze and the waning moon. From now on, even with the beautiful moments and scenic views, they will seem meaningless. Even if there are thousands of feelings in my heart, whom can I share them with?

《水调歌头·明月几时有》
（苏轼）

明月几时有？把酒问青天。不知天上宫阙，今夕是何年。我欲乘风归去，又恐琼楼玉宇，高处不胜寒。起舞弄清影，何似在人间？

转朱阁，低绮户，照无眠。不应有恨，何事长向别时圆？人有悲欢离合，月有阴晴圆缺，此事古难全。但愿人长久，千里共婵娟。

 参考译文

明月何时才出现？举杯问青天。不知天上的宫殿，此刻是哪一年。我想乘风回到天上，但又害怕那高处美玉砌成的宫阙中寒冷难耐。翩翩起舞玩赏着月下清影，人间生活其实更有乐趣。

月光照亮了朱红色的阁楼和雕花的窗户，照在睡不着的人身上。月亮不应该对人有怨恨吧？可为什么总是在人离别时才圆？人有悲欢离合的变迁，月亮有阴晴圆缺的转换，这些都是古往今来难以避免的事情。只愿我们能长久健康，即使相隔千里，也能共享这美好的月光。

When will the bright moon appear? I raise my cup and ask the sky. I wonder, in the heavenly palace, what year this night might be. I wish to ride the wind and return to the celestial realm, yet I fear the jade towers and crystal palaces, for such heights are too cold to bear. As I dance with my shadow in the moonlight, I find that life on earth is actually more enjoyable.

The moonlight shines on the vermilion mansion, filters through the carved windows, and shines on those who are sleepless. The moon should not bear resentment towards people. Why must the moon always be full when we are apart? People have their sorrows, joys, partings, and reunions; the moon has its dimness, brightness, waxing, and waning—these things have never been perfect since ancient times. I only wish we could live long and share this beautiful moonlight, though a thousand miles apart.

《如梦令·昨夜雨疏风骤》

（李清照）

昨夜雨疏风骤，浓睡不消残酒。试问卷帘人，却道海棠依旧。知否，知否？应是绿肥红瘦。

 **参考译文**

昨夜雨虽然下得稀疏，风却刮得急猛，我沉沉地睡着，醒来时还有酒意未消。问正在卷帘子的侍女，她说海棠花还是和昨天一样。你知道吗？其实那花应该是绿叶繁茂，红花凋零了。

Last night, the rain was sparse, but the wind blew fiercely. Even after a deep sleep, I still had the lingering effects of the wine. I asked the maid rolling up the curtains, and she replied that the begonias were still the same. Don't you know, don't you know? It should be that the green leaves are flourishing, while the red flowers fading.

《破阵子·为陈同甫赋壮词以寄之》
（辛弃疾）

醉里挑灯看剑，梦回吹角连营。八百里分麾下炙，五十弦翻塞外声，沙场秋点兵。

马作的卢飞快，弓如霹雳弦惊。了却君王天下事，赢得生前身后名。可怜白发生！

 参考译文

喝醉了挑亮油灯观看宝剑，梦中回到战场听到号角声响。将军分赏烤牛肉给士兵，军中乐器奏出激烈的战曲。这是秋天在战场上阅兵。

战马像的卢马一样飞驰，弓弦发出的声音像惊雷一样响亮。我一心想为君王完成收复国家失地的大业，赢得生前死后的美名。一梦醒来，可惜现在已是白发苍苍。

Drunk, I lit the lamp to look at my sword; in dreams, I heard the bugle sounding through the camps. The roast beef was shared among the soldiers, and the military instruments played the battle songs. On the autumn battlefield, the troops were inspected.

The horses gallop as fast as the famous steed Dilu, and the bowstring snaps like thunder. I am wholeheartedly determined to help the emperor complete the great cause of reclaiming the lost territories of our country, and win fame both during my lifetime and after my death. Alas, now I find myself with only gray hair when I wake up from this dream!

课 后练习

1. 选择题：庆历新政的主导者是谁？

A. 王安石

B. 范仲淹

C. 欧阳修

D. 富弼

2. 判断题：王安石变法成功地减轻了民众的经济负担。

3. 填空题：庆历新政始于____年，涉及的领域包括政治、经济、军事、社会及文化。

4. 简答题："庆历新政"实施期间所面临的主要挑战是什么？

5. 讨论题：王安石变法如何影响宋朝的政治和社会结构，并分析其长远影响。

课 文参考翻译

During the Qingli period of Emperor Renzong of the Song Dynasty and the Xining period of Emperor Shenzong of the Song Dynasty, there were two significant reform movements.

The "New Politics during Qingli Period," initiated by Emperor Renzong of the Northern Song Dynasty was a political reform led by Fan Zhongyan aimed at saving the Song Dynasty from crisis, strengthening the nation and its military. Starting in 1043, this reform ended in 1045 when Fan Zhongyan, Han Qi, Fu Bi, Ouyang Xiu and other people were ostracized from the court. The reform encompassed various areas including politics, economics, military affairs, society, and culture, focusing primarily on restructuring the bureaucracy, reducing redundant officials and troops, and addressing fiscal waste. During the reform period, a stringent assessment system was employed to remove incompetent or corrupt officials, and capable bureaucrats were promoted to key positions, which significantly improved administrative efficiency and the financial situation. Key economic indicators, like grain transportation, also improved, and the political situation began to show initial signs of recovery. However, after the implementation of the New Politics, the privilege of obtaining official positions through family connections decreased, and the evaluation and promotion system became more stringent. The discussion accusing Fan Zhongyan of forming a "clique" resurfaced. Eventually, Fan Zhongyan and others were successively removed from their positiens, and various reform measures were also abolished. The "New Politics during Qingli Period" ended in failure. The New Politics not only left the political and social issues unresolved, but its failure exacerbated land annexation, increased the fiscal burden, and sharpened social and ethnic conflicts, becoming the direct impetus for Wang Anshi's Reform under Emperor Shenzong of Song Dynasty.

Wang Anshi's Reform, known as the "Xining Reform" or the "Xifeng Reform," commenced in 1069 during Emperor Shenzong's reign and ended with his death in 1085. Aimed at strengthening the military and boosting production, the reform focused on financial management and military restructuring. This was another large-scale political reform in the history of ancient China following "Wang Mang's Reform." Despite increasing government revenue and advancing military reforms, implementation issues led to heavier burdens on the populace and intensified conflicts between new and old political factions. Wang Anshi resigned from the position of prime minister twice due to internal pressures, but with the support of Emperor Shenzong, the Reform was still basically implemented. After Shenzong passed away, the reform was largely repealed when Empress Dowager Xuanren and Sima Guang rose to power, marking the near-complete rollback of Wang Anshi's policies.

第二课

宋朝时期的法律（二）

课 前准备

　　宋朝的法律形式，除保留唐朝的律、令、格、式之外，还将敕与例作为重要的法律形式，编敕与编例成为重要的立法活动。建隆四年（963 年），宋太祖令工部尚书窦仪主持修律，完成了《宋建隆重详定刑统》，简称《宋刑统》。《宋刑统》是宋朝最基本的法典，也是中国历史上第一部刊版印行的法典，其效力一直延续到南宋，在宋朝法律史上占有重要地位。[1]

图 2-1　河南开封：开封府[2]

During the Song Dynasty, in addition to retaining the Tang Dynasty's statutes, decrees, regulations, and protocols, imperial orders and examples were also established as important legal forms, with the compilation of imperial orders and examples becoming significant legislative activities. In the fourth

---

　　[1]　参见朱勇主编：《中国法律史》，中国政法大学出版社 2021 年版，第 197 页。

　　[2]　"开封府"又称"南衙"，初建于五代时期梁开平元年（907 年），由于战火毁损和黄河水淹，昔日的开封府早已无存。图中现存的开封府景区是以宋代开封府衙为原型修建的文化游览区。

year of Jianlong (963), Emperor Taizu of Song instructed Dou Yi, the Minister of the Ministry of Works, to oversee the revision of laws, resulting in the "Retailed Criminal Code During the Jianlong era of Song Dynasty," commonly known as the "Criminal Code of Song Dynasty." The "Criminal Code of Song Dynasty" was the most fundamental code of laws during the Song Dynasty and the first codex in Chinese history to be printed and published. Its validity continued into the Southern Song Dynasty, holding a significant place in the legal history of the Song Dynasty.

 生词表

序号	生词	词性	汉语拼音	英文解释
1	敕	*n.*	chì	imperial order
2	例	*n.*	lì	example，precedent
3	编敕	*v.*	biān chì	compile imperial orders
4	编例	*v.*	biān lì	compile examples
5	尚书	*n.*	shàng shū	a high-ranking official
6	修律	*v.*	xiū lǜ	revise laws
7	刊版	*v.*	kān bǎn	cut blocks for printing
8	印行	*v.*	yìn xíng	print and punish

 导　读

　　《宋刑统》继承《唐律疏议》12 篇的体例，并在此基础上进行创新，主要表现在以下几个方面：①法典改变了自商鞅"改法为律"以来的历代传统，不再称"律"，而称"刑统"；②把唐开元二年（714 年）以来直到宋太祖建隆三年（962 年）近 250 年间的敕、令、格、式中，有关刑事法律规范的 177 条，按照时间先后顺序，分门别类地附在律文之后；③开创性地新增"臣等起请"之条，作为向朝廷提出的修改建议；④首创综合性法规之门和具有类

推适用性质的"余条准此"，附在《名例律》之后，对于司法人员检用法律、避免贻误起到很大作用；⑤《宋刑统·名例律》有20条疏议增加新的内容，并在新增内容的前面，冠以"议"字。[1]

图 2-2　北宋·《御笔手诏碑》[2]

---

〔1〕 参见朱勇主编：《中国法律史》，中国政法大学出版社 2021 年版，第 197~199 页。

〔2〕 转引自《法制文物日历 | 三月二十八日·北宋·〈御笔手诏碑〉》，载"中国政法大学法律古籍整理研究所"公众号 2023 年 3 月 28 日，https://mp.weixin.qq.com/s/RSPUINfP10bH_COV5b1-dQ，最后访问日期：2025 年 5 月 30 日。

唐宋时期是中国传统法制发展的高峰，其中一个很重要的原因就是唐宋的统治者对于法律的作用有充分的认识。在这一点上，宋朝尤为突出，这主要体现在如下几个方面：

第一，宋王朝的最高统治者十分重视法制的作用。例如，宋太祖曾下诏：**"王者禁人为非，乃设法令。"**（《宋史纪事本末》）北宋时期前后几代皇帝都能够深刻认识法律的作用，并致力于立法建设，这在中国古代是难能可贵的。

第二，重视培养官吏的法律素养。除了在科举考试中把法律作为重要内容，在各级官员中间，也形成了学法知法的政治导向。宋神宗时，**"进士及第自第一人以下注官，并先试律令、大义、断案"**（《续资治通鉴长编》）。

第三，注重总结司法经验。在宋朝时期，郑克的《折狱龟鉴》和宋慈的《洗冤集录》相继问世。《折狱龟鉴》是中国现存最早汇编有关决狱、检验的案例并加以分析评述的著作，是研究中国古代司法活动的重要参考文献。《洗冤集录》则是宋慈结合自己的实践经验，对于中国古代法医学成果的全面总结，一经问世，就被钦命颁行全国，成为南宋决狱官员的必读之书，更被后世司法官吏奉为权威。

在吸取了唐王朝因为藩镇割据走向历史衰败的经验教训之后，宋王朝统治者同时采取了一系列加强中央集权的措施：在军事上回收兵权；在行政体制上，调整中央管理机构的设置，分割地方行政职权；在职官任免上，实行实际官名与实际职务分离的差遣制度，分割各级长官的权力。[1]

 生词表

序号	生词	词性	汉语拼音	英文解释
1	官吏	*n.*	guān lì	officials
2	法律素养	*n.*	fǎ lǜ sù yǎng	legal literacy
3	科举	*n.*	kē jǔ	imperial examination

---

〔1〕 参见朱勇主编：《中国法律史》，中国政法大学出版社 2021 年版，第 200~202 页。

续表

序号	生词	词性	汉语拼音	英文解释
4	进士及第	*phr.*	jìn shì jí dì	passing the imperial examination and attain the degree of Jinshi
5	注官	*v.*	zhù guān	review the qualifications of officials and determine their ranks and positions based on their abilities and achievements
6	大义	*n.*	dà yì	(in this article it refers to) the legal provisions
7	断案	*v.*	duàn àn	adjudicate，make a judgment
8	行政体制	*n.*	xíng zhèng tǐ zhì	administrative system
9	分割	*v.*	fēn gē	divide，partition
10	职官任免	*phr.*	zhí guān rèn miǎn	appointment and dismissal of officials
11	差遣制度	*n.*	chāi qiǎn zhì dù	a dispatch system where official titles were seperated from actual duties

重 点汉字【礼】

"礼"，最初写为"豊"，最早出现在商代甲骨文中，表示在祭祀活动中敬奉美玉，击鼓敬神。后来词义逐渐发展，用作表达敬意，如礼待。

甲骨文中的"豊"上部像许多打着绳结的玉串，下部是一个象征鼓的形状，反映了古代用玉和鼓作为祭祀的重要元素。战国时期，"豊"演变为"禮"，加入了偏旁"示"，突出与神祭活动的联系。在小篆中，"豊"的字形更为规范，隶书则进一步简化。现代简体汉字中，"禮"被写为"礼"，更便于书写与识别。"礼"的意义也从严肃的祭祀扩展到一般的敬意表达和各种社会仪式，如婚礼、典礼。在中国古代，"礼"是道德规范和社会秩序的重要组成部分，而礼部作为中央政府机构之一负责相关事务。

图 2-3　"礼"字篆刻（王琦 刻）

礼，还可用作表示礼物，如"千里送鹅毛，礼轻情意重"，表达了即使是小礼物也能传递深厚的情感。

 汉字拓展

序号	词汇	汉语拼音	英文解释	例句
1	礼貌	lǐ mào	politeness	请你说话时保持礼貌。
2	礼服	lǐ fú	formal dress	他穿着一套黑色礼服出席晚宴。
3	礼品	lǐ pǐn	gift	会议结束时，主办方分发了礼品。
4	礼节	lǐ jié	ceremonial	他对外交礼节非常熟悉。
5	礼拜	lǐ bài	week,worship	每个礼拜天，他都会去教堂做礼拜。
6	礼堂	lǐ táng	auditorium	毕业典礼将在学校礼堂举行。
7	礼数	lǐ shù	proper conduct	在正式场合，遵守礼数是必须的。
8	礼赞	lǐ zàn	praise	这首诗是对春天的礼赞。
9	礼帽	lǐ mào	ceremonial hat	他戴上礼帽，显得非常英俊。
10	礼尚往来	lǐ shàng wǎng lái	courtesy demands reciprocity	我们应该做到礼尚往来，互相尊重。
11	礼金	lǐ jīn	monetary gift	婚礼上，来宾通常会送上礼金。

续表

序号	词汇	汉语拼音	英文解释	例句
12	礼教	lǐ jiào	Confucian code of ethics	他深受传统礼教的影响。
13	典礼	diǎn lǐ	ceremony	开幕式是一场盛大的典礼。

 化知识【唐宋八大家】

图 2-4　山东青州：欧阳修纪念馆

　　唐宋八大家，是唐代和宋代八位散文家的合称，又被称为"唐宋散文八大家"，分别为唐代的韩愈、柳宗元和宋代的欧阳修、苏洵、苏轼、苏辙、王安石、曾巩八位。其中，韩愈、柳宗元是唐代古文运动的领袖，欧阳修、苏洵、苏轼、苏辙等四人是宋代古文运动的核心人物。苏洵、苏轼、苏辙为父子兄弟三人，人称"三苏"，有"一门三学士"之赞誉。王安石和曾巩则是临川文学的代表人物。他们先后掀起古文运动浪潮，使诗文发展的陈旧面貌焕然一新。明初朱右选韩愈、柳宗元等八人的文章编做《八先生文集》，从此开始用八大家之名。

韩愈（768 年～824 年）：唐代著名文学家、思想家、教育家，主张"文以载道"，强调文章应该为社会服务，反对六朝骈文的形式主义，提倡古文，注重文章的内容和思想性。

柳宗元（773 年～819 年）：唐代文学家、哲学家，与韩愈并称"韩柳"，唐代古文运动的重要推动者之一。柳宗元的散文语言精练，富有哲理，尤其擅长游记和寓言，代表作有《小石潭记》《捕蛇者说》等。

欧阳修（1007 年～1072 年）：北宋时期的文学家、史学家、政治家，宋代古文运动的领袖之一，提倡文章应简洁流畅，反对形式主义的骈文，代表作包括《醉翁亭记》《秋声赋》等。

苏洵（1009 年～1066 年）：北宋文学家，苏轼和苏辙的父亲，世称"老苏"。苏洵的散文以议论为主，逻辑严密，风格雄健有力，代表作如《权书》《六国论》等。

苏轼（1037 年～1101 年）：北宋著名文学家、书画家、政治家，"唐宋八大家"中最为著名的人物之一。苏轼在诗、词、文等多方面都有卓越的成就。他的作品思想深刻、感情真挚、语言生动，代表作有《赤壁赋》《后赤壁赋》等。

苏辙（1039 年～1112 年）：北宋文学家，苏洵之子，苏轼之弟，与父兄并称"三苏"。苏辙的散文朴实无华，注重说理，代表作有《黄州快哉亭记》等。

王安石（1021 年～1086 年）：北宋著名的政治家、文学家、改革家。王安石是北宋变法运动的领导者之一，同时也是一位出色的散文家。王安石的文章内容充实、逻辑严密，语言简洁有力，代表作有《答司马谏议书》《游褒禅山记》等。

曾巩（1019 年～1083 年）：北宋文学家，欧阳修的学生，宋代古文运动的重要人物之一。曾巩的散文风格平易近人、结构严谨、内容充实，代表作有《墨池记》《寄欧阳舍人书》等。

"唐宋八大家"在中国文学史上的地位极为重要，他们的散文创作不仅革新了文体风格，使古文焕发出新的生命力，同时也通过文章表达了其对社会、政治和人生的思考，影响了后世众多文人。通过他们的努力，唐宋时期的古文创作达到了新的高度，为后代的文学创作树立了典范。

法 治文物【《宋真宗文臣七条戒官吏碑》】

宋代建中靖国元年（1101年），宋徽宗将真宗皇帝御书的"文臣七条箴言"刻成箴言碑，世称《宋真宗文臣七条戒官吏碑》，由绛州知州时恪立石。石碑嵌于绛州大堂（今山西省新绛县），时时勉励为政百官。碑高116厘米，宽70厘米，嵌于大堂壁间。碑四周刻缠枝莲花纹，中间大小字并列。

图 2-5 《宋真宗文臣七条戒官吏碑》[1]

碑文载"真宗皇帝大中祥符二年作《文臣七条》，彝伦攸叙，敷锡庶官。

---

〔1〕 参见《北宋·〈宋真宗文臣七条戒官吏〉》，载中国政法大学中华法制文明虚拟博物馆，https://flgj.cupl.edu.cn/info/1072/4087.htm，最后访问日期：2025年3月11日。

恭刻坚珉，昭示万世，仰遵圣训焉"。"七条"分别为清心、奉公、修德、责实、明察、劝课、革弊，每条下均附简要说明。

《赤壁赋》

　　壬戌之秋，七月既望，苏子与客泛舟游于赤壁之下。清风徐来，水波不兴。举酒属客，诵明月之诗，歌窈窕之章。少焉，月出于东山之上，徘徊于斗牛之间。白露横江，水光接天。纵一苇之所如，凌万顷之茫然。浩浩乎如冯虚御风，而不知其所止；飘飘乎如遗世独立，羽化而登仙。

图 2-6　南宋·青绿本《赤壁图》

　　于是饮酒乐甚，扣舷而歌之。歌曰："桂棹兮兰桨，击空明兮溯流光。渺渺兮予怀，望美人兮天一方。"客有吹洞箫者，倚歌而和之。其声呜呜然，如怨如慕，如泣如诉，余音袅袅，不绝如缕。舞幽壑之潜蛟，泣孤舟之嫠妇。

苏子愀然，正襟危坐而问客曰："何为其然也？"客曰："'月明星稀，乌鹊南飞'，此非曹孟德之诗乎？西望夏口，东望武昌，山川相缪，郁乎苍苍，此非孟德之困于周郎者乎？方其破荆州，下江陵，顺流而东也，舳舻千里，旌旗蔽空，酾酒临江，横槊赋诗，固一世之雄也，而今安在哉？况吾与子渔樵于江渚之上，侣鱼虾而友麋鹿，驾一叶之扁舟，举匏樽以相属。寄蜉蝣于天地，渺沧海之一粟。哀吾生之须臾，羡长江之无穷。挟飞仙以遨游，抱明月而长终。知不可乎骤得，托遗响于悲风。"

苏子曰："客亦知夫水与月乎？逝者如斯，而未尝往也；盈虚者如彼，而卒莫消长也。盖将自其变者而观之，则天地曾不能以一瞬；自其不变者而观之，则物与我皆无尽也，而又何羡乎！且夫天地之间，物各有主，苟非吾之所有，虽一毫而莫取。惟江上之清风，与山间之明月，耳得之而为声，目遇之而成色，取之无禁，用之不竭，是造物者之无尽藏也，而吾与子之所共适。"

客喜而笑，洗盏更酌。肴核既尽，杯盘狼藉。相与枕藉乎舟中，不知东方之既白。

 参考译文

在壬戌年的秋天，七月十六日，苏轼和朋友一起在赤壁下泛舟游玩。微风徐徐吹来，水面平静未起波澜。他们一边举杯相邀，一边吟诵赞美明月的诗歌，歌颂美丽恬静的景象。不久，月亮从东山之上升起，缓缓移动在斗宿和牛宿之间。白茫茫的雾气横贯江面，清冷冷的水光连着天际。他们随意划船，在茫茫的水面上遨游，心情豁然开朗，如同驾云御风，自由自在，忘记了归途；飘飘摇摇好像要离开尘世飘飞而起，羽化成仙，进入仙境。

于是，他们欢饮之余，敲船舷而歌唱。歌中唱道："桂木为棹，兰草为桨，击打着月光下的清波，逆流而上。我心茫茫，望着天边的佳人。"有客人吹起洞箫，依着歌声伴奏。箫声低沉哀婉，如同含情脉脉，又如悲泣诉说，余音在江上回荡，像细丝一样缭绕不绝。可使深山幽谷中的蛟龙舞动，令孤舟上的寡妇哭泣。

苏轼感到惆怅，整理衣冠端坐向客人询问："箫声为何会如此哀怨呢？"客人回答："'月明星稀，乌鹊南飞'，这不是曹操的诗吗？此处向西望是夏口，向东望是武昌，山川相连，景色郁郁葱葱，这不正是曹操在周瑜包围下的窘境吗？当年曹操破了荆州，夺得江陵，顺流而东，千里船队，旗帜遮天，临江饮酒，横执长矛吟诗，曾是一时的英雄，但现在他又在哪里呢？何况我和你在江上钓鱼砍柴，与鱼虾为伴，与鹿为友，驾着小船，举杯相约。我们仿佛是天地间的一只蜉蝣，沧海中的一粒粟米。不由哀叹我们的一生只是短暂的片刻，而羡慕长江的永恒。希望与飞仙遨游，与明月共存。明知难以一蹴而就，却将遗憾化为箫音寄托于哀风之中。"

苏轼说："客人也知道水和月亮的道理吗？过去的就像那流水一样，其实并没有真正逝去；满和缺像那月亮一样，永远在变换中保持不变。如果从变化的角度看，天地也不能停留片刻；如果从不变的角度看，万物和我都是永恒的，还有什么好羡慕的！在天地之间，万物各有其主，若非我所有，哪怕一毫也不可取。唯有江上的清风和山间的明月，听得见的变成声音，看得见的变成色彩，随取不尽，用之不竭，这是造物者给我们的无限宝藏，我和你正共同享受这一切。"

客人听后高兴地笑了，洗净酒杯继续畅饮。饭食已尽，杯盘凌乱。他们在船上互相枕着垫着睡去，不知不觉中东方已经泛白。

In the autumn of the year Renxu, on the 16th day of July, Su Shi and his friend boated for pleasure beneath the Red Cliff. A gentle breeze wafted in, and the water remained calm. They raised their cups to each other, reciting poems about the bright moon and singing verses about serene beauty. Soon, the moon rose above the eastern mountains, wandering between the constellations of Dou and Niu. White mist heaped up across the river, and the water's gleam merged with the sky. With a single oar, they traversed the vastness as if riding the wind through emptiness, unaware of their destination; they floated as if they had left the world behind, ready to ascend to immortality.

Thus, they drank and were merry, tapping on the boat's side to the rhythm of their song. The song went: "With oars of cassia and paddles of orchid, we strike the clear waves in the moonlight and sail upstream. Vast is my longing, looking for my beloved in the distant sky." A guest played the vertical bamboo flute, accompanying the song. The sound was mournful, like longing, like sorrow, like grief, like lamentation. The lingering sound echoed over the river, lingering like the silk threads that tapered off endlessly. The sound could make the dragons in deep valleys dance and make a widow on the lonely boat weep.

Su Shi grew melancholic. He adjusted his clothes and sat up straight, asking the guest, "Why is the sound of the flute so mournful?" The guest replied, "Is this not Cao Cao's poem where he mentions 'the moonlit sky and the southward flight of crows'? Looking west from here to Xiakou and east to Wuchang, the landscapes blend into each other, lush and vast. Isn't this reminiscent of Cao Cao surrounded by Zhou Yu's forces? When he conquered Jingzhou, took Jiangling, and traveled down the river, his fleets stretched for miles, his banners covered the skies. He drank wine facing the river, and composed poems while holding a lance horizontally, truly a hero of his time. Yet, where is he now? Moreover, here we are, fishing and gathering firewood on the river islets, taking fish and shrimp as companions and elk as friends.We steer a leaf-like skiff, raising a gourd cup to toast each other. We are like mayflies in the cosmos, mere specks in the vast ocean. We lament our fleeting lives and envy the endless flow of the Yangtze. We wish to travel with immortals and accompany the moon eternally. Knowing such sudden achievements are unattainable, I leave our lingering thoughts in the sorrowful wind."

Su Shi said, "Do you also understand the way of water and the moon? The past is like this river. In fact, it hasn't truly disappeared. Waxing and waning are like the moon, endlessly cycling without cessation, but never out of its sphere. If we observe from the perspective of change, even heaven and earth cannot pause for a moment; if we observe from the perspective of constancy, all things and I are eternal. What then is there to envy? Moreover, between heaven and earth, everything has its owner. If it is not mine, I shall not take even a bit. Only the clear winds above the river and the bright moon between the mountains can be turned into sounds when heard and colours when seen, acquired without restriction, used without depletion. They are the inexhaustible treasures bestowed by the Creator, which you and I rightly share."

The guest laughed joyfully in response, washed the cups, and poured more drink. After the meal was finished, the plates and cups were in disarray. Together, they reclined in the boat; unknowingly, the sky in the east had already turned white.

课 **后练习**

1. 选择题：宋朝司法经验的总结体现在以下哪位作者的作品中？

A. 郑克的《折狱龟鉴》

B. 宋慈的《洗冤集录》

C. 两者都是

D. 以上都不是

2. 判断题：宋朝的最高统治者，并不重视法制的作用。

3. 填空题：宋神宗时期的科举考试中，考生任官职前需要先试的三个内容是_____、_____和_____。

4. 简答题：请简述宋慈的《洗冤集录》对后世法医学和司法实践的影响。

5. 讨论题：宋朝在唐朝藩镇割据导致灭亡的历史教训基础上，如何通过加强中央集权来避免同样的命运。

课 **文参考翻译**

During the Tang and Song Dynasties, China experienced a peak in the development of its traditional legal system, with a significant reason being the rulers' comprehensive understanding of the role of law, particularly during the Song Dynasty.

This was mainly reflected in several aspects:

First, the highest rulers of the Song Dynasty greatly emphasized the role of legal systems. For instance, Emperor Taizu of Song once stated: "For a ruler to prohibit people from wrongdoing, there are laws and decrees," as recorded in *History of Song Dynasty*. Successive emperors during the Northern Song Dynasty deeply recognized the importance of law and were dedicated to legislative construction, which is a commendable feat in ancient China.

Second, there was a focus on cultivating legal literacy among officials. In addition to including law as a crucial subject in the imperial examination, there was also a political orientation towards learning and understanding law among officials at all levels. During the reign of Emperor Shenzong of Song, it was decreed that "those who passed the imperial examinations, from the top scorer downwards, were appointed officials only after being tested on laws, principles, and case adjudication," as recorded in *Supplement to Historical Mirror to Aid in Government*.

Third, there was an emphasis on summarizing judicial experience.During the Song Dynasty, Zheng Ke's *Mirror for Adjudication* and Song Ci's *Records of Redressing Grievances* were successively published. The *Mirror for Adjudication* was China's earliest existing work to collect and analyze historical cases related to adjudication and inspection, serving as an important reference for studying ancient Chinese judicial activities. *Records of Redressing Grievances* by Song Ci was a comprehensive summary of ancient Chinese forensic achievements based on his practical experience. Once published, it was officially disseminated throughout the country by imperial decree, becoming essential reading for adjudication officials in the Southern Song Dynasty, and was revered by judicial officials in later generations as authoritative.

After drawing lessons from the historical decline of the Tang Dynasty due to regional military insurrections, the Song rulers implemented a series of measures to strengthen centralization. In the military, the emperors reduced military powers among regional commanders; in the administrative system, they adjusted the setup of central administrative organs and divided local administrative powers; in official appointments, they implemented a system where official titles were separated from actual duties to distribute power among various levels of officials.

第三课

宋朝时期的法律（三）

课 前准备

图 3-1　北宋·《清明上河图》（局部）（张择端）

　　宋朝初年，经济由萧条、凋敝到复苏、繁荣，阶级结构发生深刻变化，随着立契租佃制度的普遍确立，客户[1]及手工业者等人与生产资料所有者的主家的人身依附关系日趋松散。商品经济的繁荣及私有制的深化，使私有财产（包括小生产者的私有权益）的占有、收益、处分以及典当、担保、继承、婚姻、负债等民事法律关系的发生更加频繁。

　　与之相适应，宋朝的民事法律呈现出如下特点：民事权利主体的范围扩大，对行为能力的规定有所发展；民事立法多以单行法的形式出现，在物权、债负、婚姻、财产继承等方面，比唐律更加完善；等等。[2]

At the onset of the Song Dynasty, the economy transitioned from depression and decay to recovery and prosperity, leading to significant changes in class structure. With the widespread establishment of the tenancy by contract system, the personal dependencies of tenants and craftsmen, and other people on one hand, and the masters who were the owners of the means of pro-

---

〔1〕"客户"在此指没有土地的人，与拥有土地的"主户"相对应。
〔2〕参见朱勇主编：《中国法律史》，中国政法大学出版社 2021 年版，第 206 页。

duction on the other hand, began to loosen. The flourishing of the commodity economy and the deepening of private ownership resulted in more frequent occurrences of civil legal relationships related to the possession, profit, disposal, pawning, guarantee, inheritance, marriage, and debt of private property, including the private rights and interests of small producers.

In response to these changes, the civil law of the Song Dynasty demonstrated the following characteristics: The scope of subjects with civil rights expanded, and regulations regarding capacity for civil conduct were further developed; civil legislation often appeared in the form of separate statutes, providing more comprehensive provisions on aspects such as property rights, debt, marriage, inheritance, than those of the Tang Dynasty; and so on.

 生词表

序号	生词	词性	汉语拼音	英文解释
1	萧条	*adj.*	xiāo tiáo	depressed，sluggish
2	凋敝	*adj.*	diāo bì	decayed，destitute
3	租佃制度	*n.*	zū diàn zhì dù	tenancy system
4	依附关系	*phr.*	yī fù guān xì	dependency relationship
5	松散	*adj.*	sōng sǎn	loose
6	商品经济	*n.*	shāng pǐn jīng jì	market economy
7	典当	*v.*	diǎn dàng	pawn
8	担保	*v.*	dān bǎo	guarantee，assure
9	行为能力	*n.*	xíng wéi néng lì	capacity for conduct，behavioral competence

 导 读

　　宋朝时，法律上的所有权已经区分为不动产所有权和动产所有权。不动

产主要指田宅，宋朝时称为"产""业"，所有权人为"业主"。动产包括六畜、奴婢，有时也包括附着于土地的矿物、植物，还包括货币及有价证券等，这些被称为物或财物，它们的所有权又称"物主权"。

图 3-2　故宫博物院：北宋·钧窑玫瑰紫釉葵花式花盆

《宋刑统·户婚律》规定：**"器物之属，须移徙其地……地既不离常处，理与财物有殊，"**可见，宋朝在法律上区分动产与不动产。

宋朝法律中的不动产主要是指土地，土地买卖、土地所有权是法律的重要内容，史称**"官中条令，惟交易一事最为详备"**（《袁氏世范》）。随着封建社会后期商品经济的发展，唐朝的均田制以及其他形式的国家土地所有制日趋式微，地主土地私有制迅速发展，特别是宋朝"不立田制""不抑兼并"，允许官僚、地主以经济手段任意购置、兼并土地，甚至国家也作为交易主体参与其中。在法律上，宋朝承认百姓对于新垦荒田的所有权。对于战乱、灾荒之后的弃田，两宋均规定耕种者可以享有事实上的占有，在其占有的前几年内减免税赋，如果十年内原主不来复业，则官府承认占有者对土地的所有权，换言之，弃田土地所有权的取得时效为十年。通过买卖取得的不动产所有权，以官契作为合法的产权证书。法律规定，不动产所有权的转移必须经过官府承认，缴纳契税，然后由官府在买卖契约上加盖公章，称为"红契"，又称"赤契"。红契既是已纳税的标志，又是土地所有权的凭证，一旦发生争讼，就是不容置疑的证据。但在实际生活中，买卖双方的当事人为规避契税，往往私立草契，以白契成交。[1]

 生词表

序号	生词	词性	汉语拼音	英文解释
1	不动产	n.	bù dòng chǎn	real estate，immovable property
2	动产	n.	dòng chǎn	personal property，movable property
3	业主	n.	yè zhǔ	property owner
4	奴婢	n.	nú bì	slave，servant
5	有价证券	n.	yǒu jià zhèng quàn	securities
6	物主权	n.	wù zhǔ quán	ownership of goods
7	移徙	v.	yí xǐ	move，relocate
8	均田制	n.	jūn tián zhì	equal-land system
9	新垦荒田	phr.	xīn kěn huāng tián	newly reclaimed wasteland
10	弃田	n.	qì tián	abandoned land
11	占有	v.	zhàn yǒu	possess，occupy
12	减免税赋	phr.	jiǎn miǎn shuì fù	tax reduction or exemption
13	复业	v.	fù yè	resume one's occupation or business
14	土地所有权	n.	tǔ dì suǒ yǒu quán	land ownership
15	缴纳	v.	jiǎo nà	pay，hand over
16	契税	n.	qì shuì	deed tax

---

〔1〕　参见朱勇主编：《中国法律史》，中国政法大学出版社 2021 年版，第 207~208 页。

续表

序号	生词	词性	汉语拼音	英文解释
17	公章	*n.*	gōng zhāng	official seal
18	红契	*n.*	hóng qì	red deed（officially stamped deed）
19	赤契	*n.*	chì qì	another term for "红契"
20	争讼	*n.*	zhēng sòng	litigation，lawsuit
21	规避	*v.*	guī bì	evade，avoid
22	草契	*n.*	cǎo qì	informal or unofficial deed
23	白契	*n.*	bái qì	another term for "草契"

重 点汉字【比】

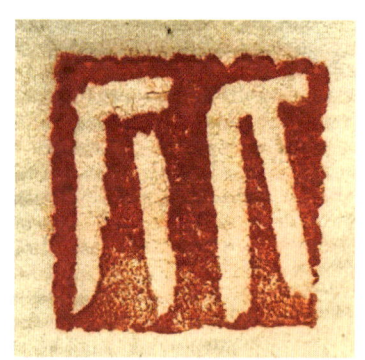

图 3-3 "比"字篆刻（王琦 刻）

　　"比"是汉语中常用的规范汉字。这个字的本义是"靠近"或"并列"，只有挨得很近才有可能进行"比较"，因此"比"也引申出了"比较"的意思。由此义进一步发展，"比"还有比喻、比方的意思，接着又有比照、仿照的含义。同时，"比"从"靠近"又引申为"密集"，再进一步引申为"接近"和"勾结"。

　　"比"字的形体最早见于商代甲骨文，金文的形体和甲骨文的结构基本一致，小篆则在此基础上规整了笔画，隶书和楷书则根据小篆进行了进一步的笔画改动。传统认为，"比"字的古文字形象是两个面朝右并排站立的人，表示"靠近"或"挨着"的意思，与"从"字的构形相似。但从甲骨文的形象来看，"比"字的构件与"人"有明显区别。"比"字应由两个"匕"组成，"匕"是古代的一种形似长柄浅勺的取食器具。两个"匕"并排组合成"比"，表示相邻、靠近的意思，同时也暗示了"比"字的发音。

也有学者认为，古文字中的"匕"与出土的匕具有较大差异，更像是模拟人站立拱手侧身的形象。有些学者据此推测，"匕"字可能是"臂"字的初始形，手臂部分特意画成弯曲状，以突出所表达的部位。两个"匕"并列构成"比"，表示两手臂并列，因此其本义为"偕同"。

 ## 汉字拓展

序号	词汇	汉语拼音	英文解释	例句
1	比较	bǐ jiào	compare	我们需要比较这两款产品的性能。
2	比例	bǐ lì	proportion	这张图表呈现了不同年龄组所占的比例。
3	比赛	bǐ sài	competition	明天我们学校将举行一场足球比赛。
4	比喻	bǐ yù	metaphor	他用一个简单的比喻解释了这个复杂的科学原理。
5	比如	bǐ rú	for instance	比如，我们可以从历史中学到很多东西。
6	对比	duì bǐ	contrast	我们对这两个案例进行了详细对比。
7	比翼双飞	bǐ yì shuāng fēi	fly side by side	他们比翼双飞，如同一对恩爱的鸟儿。
8	比重	bǐ zhòng	specific gravity	这种金属的比重比水大很多。
9	比拟	bǐ nǐ	analogy	作者用一系列精彩的比拟手法，增强了文章的表现力。
10	比起	bǐ qǐ	compared to	比起去年，他的成绩有了显著提高。
11	比画	bǐ hua	gesture	他们在讨论时不停地比画着手势。
12	比肩	bǐ jiān	be on a par with	他的成就可以与许多伟大的科学家比肩。

化知识【程朱理学】

　　程朱理学，又称为程朱道学，是宋明理学的主要派别之一，是中国宋朝时期由程颢、程颐和朱熹等学者共同发展起来的一种重要的哲学流派，也是儒学发展史上的一个重要阶段。程朱理学继承了先秦儒家思想，特别是孔孟的道德伦理观，同时吸收了佛教和道教的一些思想，并进行了改造与系统化，是宋代儒学复兴运动的核心成果之一。

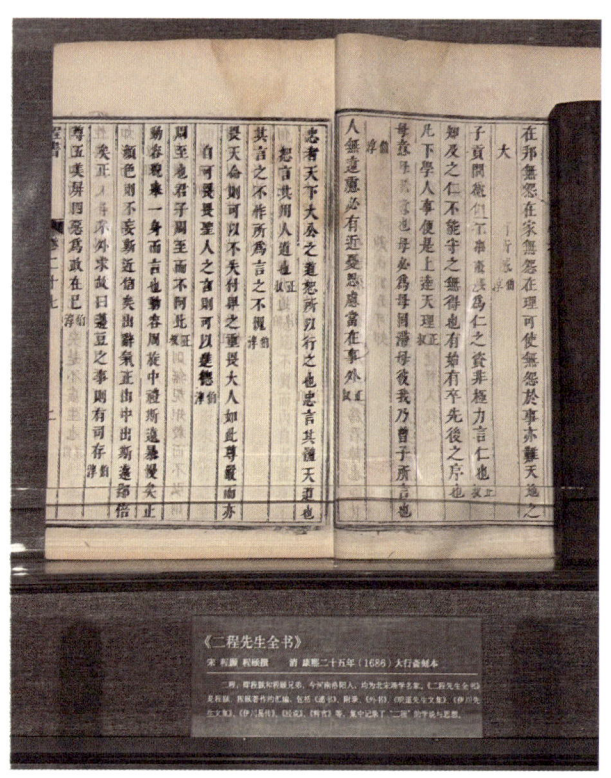

图 3-4　中国考古博物馆:《二程先生全书》清大行斋刻本

　　程朱理学的起源可以追溯到北宋时期的两位重要思想家——程颢和程颐，合称"二程"。程颢、程颐兄弟继承和发展了宋明理学开创者之一周敦颐的思想，提出了"天理"的概念，强调宇宙间存在着一种普遍的道德原则——天理，认为天理是世界的根本，是自然界和人类社会的秩序基础。他们主张通过修身养性、克己复礼来使个体与天理相契合。

到了南宋，朱熹在程颢和程颐思想的基础上，进一步发展并系统化了理学的理论。朱熹被认为是程朱理学的集大成者，他通过注解"四书"（《大学》《中庸》《论语》《孟子》）的方式，将理学的思想推广开来，其由此而创作的《四书章句集注》成为后来科举考试的标准教材。朱熹还提出了"格物致知"的学习方法，主张通过观察、思考自然和人类社会的现象来获得知识，从而最终理解天理。

程朱理学的核心思想包括"天理"、"性理"与"心性修养"。

程朱理学在南宋之后逐渐成为官方哲学，影响了中国社会的方方面面，尤其是教育和政治领域。其强调道德修养、家庭伦理和社会秩序，这些观念在当时起到了稳定社会结构的作用。程朱理学通过被吸纳进科举考试而成为国家官方意识形态，对后来元、明、清三朝的思想体系产生了深远的影响。

此外，程朱理学对日本、朝鲜和越南等东亚国家的思想发展也产生了重要影响。这些国家在接受儒学的过程中，吸收了程朱理学的思想，并将其作为教育和社会伦理的指导原则。

法 治文物【《劝慎刑文并箴》】

宋代碑铭《劝慎刑文》[1]和《慎刑箴》[2]是两篇研究宋代法制文化的重要石刻史料，两文同刻一碑，正面为《劝慎刑文》，反面为《慎刑箴》，均为北宋初年礼部尚书晁迥撰文，庞房篆额。碑文主要阐述了古代"明德慎刑"的法制思想，在文中列举了自西汉至后唐14个酷吏遭恶报的事例，以及西汉以来8例因救济人命、积有阴德而本人或子孙获福报善报的典故，以报应、因果循环事例来劝化封建统治者和为官者。

---

〔1〕 该文刻于石碑上，碑为螭首方座。碑首和碑身系整石刻制，高287厘米，宽94厘米。两面刻。碑阳额题"劝慎刑文"。碑文33行，满行61字，总1900余字。石碑正书现藏陕西省西安碑林博物馆。

〔2〕 该文刻于石碑背面，文共21行，每行44字，总820余字。

对于《劝慎刑文》和《慎刑箴》的主旨，清代金石学家王昶曾评价道："《慎刑文》述用刑善恶之报应，此碑则劝人广树阴德，而用韵语系于末。箴云'愿布斯文，置之座右'，则非对君上言矣。"

图 3-5 《劝慎刑文并箴》[1]

经 典阅读

《四书章句集注·论语集注》"学而第一"（节选）：

子曰："学而时习之，不亦说乎？[1] 有朋自远方来，不亦乐乎？[2] 人不知而不愠，不亦君子乎？[3]"

（1）学之为言效也。人性皆善，而觉有先后，后觉者必效先觉之所为，

---

〔1〕 参见《北宋·〈劝慎刑文并箴〉》，载中国政法大学中华法制文明虚拟博物馆，http://flgj.cupl. edu.cn/info/1092/4066.htm，最后访问日期：2024 年 11 月 5 日。

乃可以明善而复其初也。习，鸟数飞也。学之不已，如鸟数飞也。说，喜意也。既学而又时时习之，则所学者熟，而中心喜说，其进自不能已矣。程子曰"习，重习也。时复思绎，浃洽于中，则说也。"又曰："学者，将以行之也。时习之，则所学者在我，故说。"谢氏曰："时习者，无时而不习。坐如尸，坐时习也；立如齐，立时习也。"

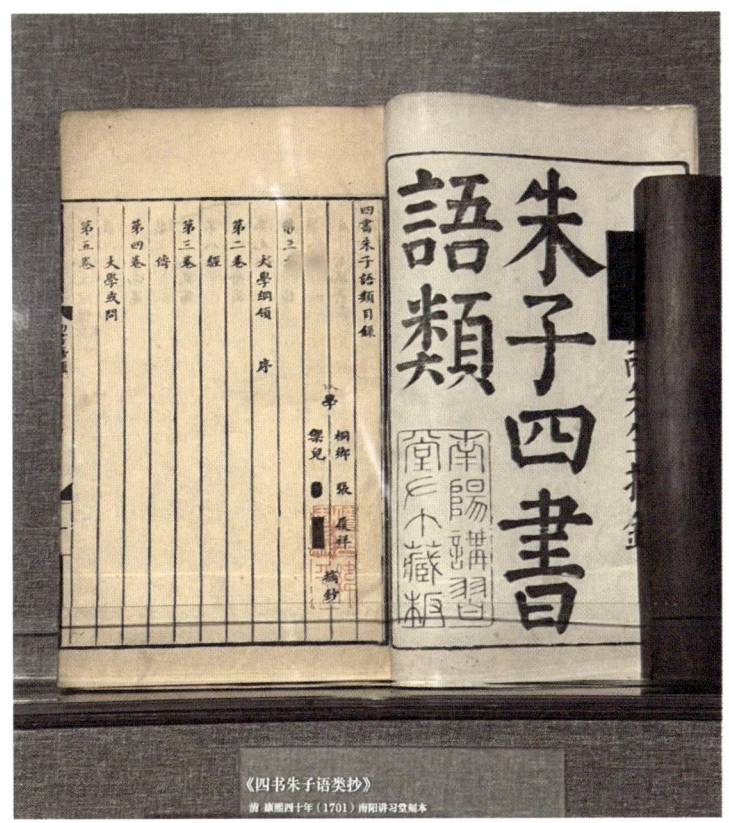

《四书朱子语类抄》

清　康熙四十年（1701）南阳讲习堂刻本

图 3-6　中国考古博物馆：《四书朱子语类抄》清南阳讲习堂刻本

（2）朋，同类也。自远方来，则近者可知。程子曰："以善及人，而信从者众，故可乐。"又曰："说在心，乐主发散在外。"

（3）愠，含怒意。君子，成德之名。尹氏曰："学在己，知不知在人，何愠之有。"程子曰："虽乐于及人，不见是而无闷，乃所谓君子。"

愚谓，及人而乐者顺而易，不知而不愠者，逆而难，故惟成德者能之。

然德之所以成，亦曰学之正、习之熟、说之深而不已焉耳。程子曰："乐由说而后得，非乐不足以语君子。"

 参考译文

孔子说："学习然后不断地复习、实践，难道不是很快乐吗？[（1）]有志同道合的朋友自远方来，不也是一件快乐的事吗？[（2）]别人不了解自己，却不因此而恼怒，不也是君子吗？[（3）]"

（1）所谓"学"，就是效仿的意思。人的本性都是善良的，但人的觉悟有先后之分，后觉悟的人必然会效仿先觉悟的人的行为，这样才能明白什么是善，并且回归到最初的纯真状态。"习"的意思是像鸟儿多次振翅飞翔一样。学习是无止境的，就像鸟儿不停地飞翔。"说"，通"悦"，指的是内心的喜悦。一旦学习了之后又不断地复习并予以实践，学到的东西就会变得熟练，内心深处感到快乐和满足，自然而然地就会不断进步。程子说："'习'是指重复学习。不断地思考和实践，让所学深入心灵，那么内心就会感到快乐。"他又说："学习是为了将来能够应用。不断地实践，那么所学的东西就真正成为自己的一部分，因此会感到快乐。"谢氏说："'时习'意味着无时无刻不在学习。坐着的时候要像祭祀中受祭的尸体那样端正，这就是坐着的时候在复习实践所学的礼仪等内容；站得像斋戒时那样恭敬，这就是站立的时候在复习实践所学的内容。"

（2）"朋"是指志同道合的人。如果有朋友从远方来（和自己交流学习），那么身边的人更容易了解到自己的为人和学问了。程子说："通过善行影响他人、传播知识，而且有很多人相信并跟从自己，因此这是可喜的。"他还说："'悦'存在于心中，而'乐'则是表现在外的状态。"

（3）"愠"的意思是含有怒意。"君子"是对具有完美德行的人的称呼。尹氏说："学习取决于自己，别人是否了解自己（的品德和学问）那是别人的事情，怎么会有怒气呢？"程子说："虽然乐于把自己的所学、所悟传播给他人，但如果不被认可也不感到沮丧，这才是所谓的君子。"

我（朱熹）认为乐于帮助他人并因此感到快乐的行为是顺其自然而容易的，而不被人理解却不生气则是违背自然而难做到的，因此只有真正具有完备德行的人才能做到。德行的成就也在于正确学习、熟练实践、内心对悦的深刻理解，并且持之以恒。程子说："快乐是由内心的喜悦得来，没有这种由内而外的快乐感受，就不足以讨论君子。"

Confucius said, "To study and then repeatedly review and practice what one has learned, isn't that also a joy? [1] Isn't it also a pleasure to have like-minded friends come from afar? [2] If one doesn't get angry when others don't understand oneself, is this not also the mark of a noble person? [3]"

（1）The so-called "学 learning" means the act of emulating. Human nature is inherently good, but people's awakenings vary in sequence. Those who awaken later will naturally emulate the actions of those who awakened earlier, thus they can understand and return to their original goodness. The meaning of "习 practice" is like birds flapping their wings several times in flight. Learning is endless, just like birds continuously flying. "说" is interchangeable with "悦", which refers to joy or delight in one's heart. If one studies and then consistently reviews and practices over time, what has been learned becomes proficient, and joy arises deep within the heart, naturally leading to continuous progress. Cheng Zi said, "'习' implies repeated practice. Constant reflection and deepening of what is learned saturate the heart, thus leading to joy." He also stated, "The purpose of learning is for its application. By continuously practicing, what is learned becomes a part of oneself, hence the joy." Xie said, "'时习 Constant practice' means practicing all the time. One should sit as upright as the sacrificial recipient during a sacrifice, which means reviewing and practicing the learned etiquette and other contents while sitting. One should stand as respectfully as when in a state of fasting, which means reviewing and practicing what one has learned while standing."

（2）"朋 Friend" refers to like-minded individuals. If friends come from afar (to communicate and study with oneself), then those nearby become easier to understand one's character and learning. Cheng Zi commented, "Extending goodness and spreading knowledge to others and being widely trusted as a result is thus joyful." He further noted, "'悦 Joy' resides in the heart, and the outward expression of '乐 happiness' disperses it externally."

（3）"愠 Anger" here implies harboring anger. "君子 Noble Person" refers to someone of perfect virtue. Yin said, "Learning depends on oneself; whether others know or do not know about one's character and learning is their business, so why harbor any anger?" Cheng Zi stated, "Even though one finds joy in reaching out to others, not being recognized yet feeling no frustration is what defines a noble person."

I（Zhu Xi）believe that helping others and deriving joy from it is a natural and easy act, while being misunderstood and yet not getting angry is against nature and difficult, hence only truly virtuous individuals can achieve this. The achievement of virtue also lies in correct learning, proficient practice, a profound understanding of inner joy, and perseverance. Cheng Zi said, "Joy comes from inner satisfaction and should not be discussed in the context of a noble person if it is lacking."

课 后练习

1. 选择题：宋朝不动产所有权的主要对象是什么？

A. 动物和奴婢

B. 土地和房产

C. 货币和有价证券

D. 矿物和植物

2. 判断题：宋朝的不动产所有权转移无需经过官府的认可。

3. 填空题：在宋朝，通过买卖取得的不动产所有权需要以_____作为合法的产权证书。

4. 简答题：宋朝如何处理战乱或灾荒后的弃田问题。

5. 讨论题：宋朝法律对动产和不动产所有权的不同处理及其背后的经济社会影响。

课 文参考翻译

"Criminal Code of Song Dynasty: Household and Marriage Laws" stipulated, "For items like 'goods' (if the crime of theft is to be established), it is necessary to move their locations... Since the land can not be moved from its usual place, hence (the relevant) principles are distinct from movable property." It can be seen that in the Song Dynasty, there was a legal distinction between movable and immovable property.

In the laws of the Song Dynasty, immovable property primarily referred to land. The sale and ownership of land were significant legal matters. As recorded in *Family Instructions of the YuanClan*: "government directives, especially detailed in transactions." With the development of the market economy in the later stages of feudal society, the Tang Dynasty's equal-field system and other forms of state land ownership declined. The private ownership of land by landlords developed rapidly, especially during the Song Dynasty, when the government did not enforce a specific land system or prevent land consolidation, allowing officials and landlords to freely purchase and consolidate land, even with state participation. Legally, the Song Dynasty recognized the people's ownership of newly reclaimed wasteland. For land abandoned due to wars or disasters, both the Northern and Southern Song stipulated that the cultivator could possess it factually, with a reduction or exemption of taxes in the initial years. If the original owner did not reclaim it within ten years, the government would recognize the possessor's rights to the land, establishing a ten-year statute of limitations for acquiring abandoned land rights. The acquisition of real property rights through sales was legitimized by official deeds, the legal certificate of property ownership. The law required that the transfer of real property rights must be recognized by the government with a deed tax paid, followed by the government stamping the sales contract with an official seal, known as the "registered deed" or "red deed." The registered deed was both a tax payment indicator and a proof of land ownership, serving as indisputable evidence in any dispute. However, in practice, to avoid deed tax, the parties involved often privately agreed on a provisional deed, completing transactions with an unofficial "white deed."

第四课

宋朝时期的法律（四）

课 前准备

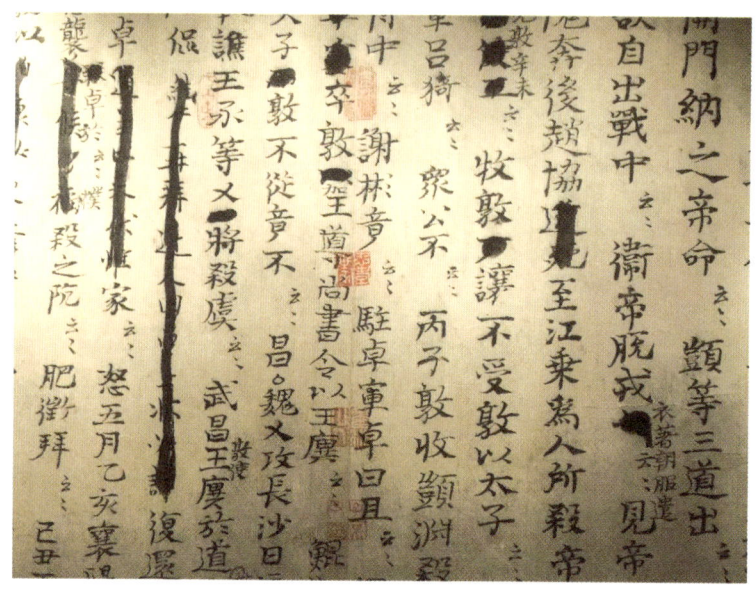

图 4-1　国家典籍博物馆：北宋·《资治通鉴》残稿（司马光）

宋朝刑事法律中的罪名和刑罚基本承袭唐律。但是由于宋朝中央集权的加强，阶级矛盾的尖锐复杂，相关立法也发生了一些重要的变化，主要表现在贼盗重法的实施和采用新的刑罚。宋朝初期，出于缓和社会矛盾、树立新统治形象的需要，宋太祖曾经采取宽政待民的政策，对一般刑事案件的处罚比较宽松，但对贼盗犯罪则一律严惩不贷。《宋史》记载：*"祖宗仁政，加于天下者甚广。刑法之重，改而从轻者至多。惟是强盗之法，特加重者，盖以禁奸宄而惠良民也。"*[1]

The criminal laws regarding offenses and penalties during the Song Dynasty largely continued the practices of the Tang laws. However, due to the

---

〔1〕　参见朱勇主编：《中国法律史》，中国政法大学出版社 2021 年版，第 203 页。

increased centralization of power and the sharp and complex class conflicts during the Song era, significant changes occurred in legislation. These changes were primarily reflected in the strict enforcement of laws against theft and the introduction of new penalties. At the founding of the Song Dynasty, to ease social tensions and establish a new image of governance, Emperor Taizu of Song adopted lenient policies towards the populace in general criminal cases. However, crimes involving theft were severely punished without exception. According to *History of Song Dynasty*, "Our ancestors' benevolent governance was extensively applied throughout the realm. Although the criminal laws were severe, many were amended to be more lenient. However, the laws against theft were specially made more stringent, aimed at prohibiting wicked acts and benefiting the good citizens."

 生词表

序号	生词	词性	汉语拼音	英文解释
1	阶级矛盾	*n.*	jiē jí máo dùn	class conflict
2	贼盗	*n.*	zéi dào	theft, robbery
3	宽政待民	*phr.*	kuān zhèng dài mín	lenient policy towards the populace
4	严惩不贷	*idm.*	yán chéng bù dài	punish severely without leniency
5	奸宄	*n.*	jiān guǐ	evildoer, malefactor

 导 读

　　宋朝贼盗罪涉及面广，内容复杂，包括谋反、叛逆、谋杀、劫囚、造畜蛊毒、造妖书妖言、强盗、窃盗、恐吓取财等多方面的犯罪。《宋刑统》所附敕文对于上述犯罪的惩罚明显重于唐律，其规定，擒获强盗，不论有赃无赃，一并集众决杀；持杖行劫，不问有赃无赃，一并处死，且其同行、同情、知

情者都同罪。然而，宋初加重刑罚的做法并没有达到预期的效果。[1]

 课 文

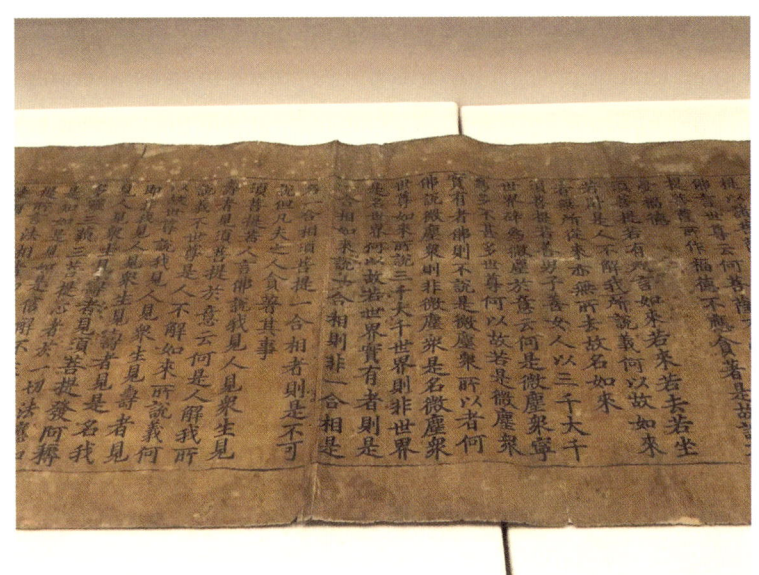

图 4-2　国家典籍博物馆：金刚般若波罗蜜经 （释鸠摩罗什 译）宋刻本

北宋中期，面对盗贼猖獗的局面，统治者愈加重视对于此类罪行的惩戒，颁布了一系列编敕，加重处罚盗贼。宋仁宗嘉祐年间，宣布对京城地区"持杖窃盗者"加重处罚；后于 1062 年颁布《窝藏重法》，这项法律把当时的京师开封府和下属的各县、相邻四州，划定为重法实施地，在此区域内窝藏盗贼的人，一律加重处罚。这种在常法之外，针对某一地区单独制定、单独适用的法律，类似于现代的刑事特别法，在中国古代是史无前例的。

宋英宗时期再一次明确，在重法地之内，对于非"十恶"范围内的强盗罪，株连家属、没收财产，这是唐律和五代法律中所没有的。

神宗时期又设立《盗贼重法》，不仅扩大了英宗时期重法地的范围，而且

---

〔1〕 参见朱勇主编：《中国法律史》，中国政法大学出版社 2021 年版，第 203~205 页。

鼓励并奖赏人们告发盗贼及窝藏盗贼的人；同时加大地方官员的捕盗责任，在非重法地犯贼盗罪也一并按照重法论处。

至宋哲宗时期，重法地涉及的范围已经占当时宋朝全国 24 个行政区划中的 17 个，《盗贼重法》在这些地区甚至完全取代了《宋刑统·贼盗律》。

但是，划定重法地、重法人，以非常之刑进行惩罚的做法，在加重了对贼盗犯罪处罚的同时，也打破了正常的法律秩序，对封建社会后期的刑罚制度产生了恶劣影响。刑罚威吓主义并不能彻底地铲除盗贼分子，贼盗犯罪反而愈治愈多，社会也愈乱。因此，北宋末年，徽宗转而实行军事镇压与抚谕招安的两手策略。

南宋时期社会形势更加紧张，统治者进一步加重对贼盗犯罪的惩治，对于免死的强盗，要在额上刺"强盗"字样，以示不齿。而两犯强盗，即使从犯也论死罪，但对饥民为盗贼者可以从轻处罚。

总之，各种因素造成了宋朝社会的结构性矛盾，而贼盗始终是宋王朝的心腹之患，纵观北宋和南宋的治理，重惩贼盗都被作为一贯的方针。[1]

 生词表

序号	生词	词性	汉语拼音	英文解释
1	猖獗	*adj.*	chāng jué	rampant，uncontrolled
2	窝藏	*v.*	wō cáng	harbor，conceal
3	划定	*v.*	huà dìng	delimit，define
4	重法	*phr.*	zhòng fǎ	severe law
5	刑事特别法	*proper n.*	Xíng shì Tè bié fǎ	special criminal law
6	株连	*v.*	zhū lián	implicate，involve others in a criminal case
7	没收	*v.*	mò shōu	confiscate

---

〔1〕 参见朱勇主编：《中国法律史》，中国政法大学出版社 2021 年版，第 203~205 页。

续表

序号	生词	词性	汉语拼音	英文解释
8	告发	v.	gào fā	report an offender，expose
9	额	n.	é	forehead
10	饥民	n.	jī mín	famine victims
11	心腹之患	idm.	xīn fù zhī huàn	major internal trouble
12	一贯	adj.	yí guàn	consistent，all along

重 点汉字【均】

图4-3 "均"字篆刻（王琦 刻）

　　"均"是汉语中的常用规范汉字，最早见于战国时期的金文，其字形演变自战国至秦代逐渐定型。《说文解字》认为"均"是形声兼会意字，表意与"土"相关，如"均"可义为一种制作陶器所用的转轮。

　　"均"在《说文解字》中被解释为"平遍"，即"无所不平"的意思，源于"土地平整"的造字本义。后来，"均"逐渐抽象化，衍生出"公平无差别"的含义，如《周礼》中负责公平分配土地的官职名称为"均人""土均"——在农业社会，将土地分给人们耕种、使用应尽量做到公平无偏差，反映在负责的官职上则称之为"均"。"均"字在现代汉语中常表示"平均、均匀"，也用作副词表示"都"，如"计划均被否决"。在古汉语中，"均"还有"等同"

和"协调"的意思。

　　古代用于确定音律的工具也叫"均"，这一意义读作"yùn"。在十二律中，以任意一律为宫建立的音阶也被称为"均"。魏晋时期为更好地体现音乐特性，另造了"韵"字，后来声韵学兴起，这个意义上的"均"字逐渐被"韵"字替代。

 汉字拓展

序号	词汇	汉语拼音	英文解释	例句
1	平均	píng jūn	average	他们的平均年龄是 30 岁。
2	均匀	jūn yún	even，uniform	请将涂料均匀地涂在墙面上。
3	均衡	jūn héng	balance	这次改革旨在实现资源分配的均衡。
4	均等	jūn děng	equal	应努力实现人人机会均等。
5	均价	jūn jià	average price	这个地区的房屋均价正在上涨。
6	均线	jūn xiàn	moving average	他用长期均线来分析股市走势。
7	均值	jūn zhí	mean value	这组数据的均值可以代表整体的水平。
8	势均力敌	shì jūn lì dí	balance of power	在这场比赛中，双方的实力势均力敌。
9	均分	jūn fēn	divide equally	奖金将被均分给团队的所有成员。
10	均可	jūn kě	all acceptable	这些选项均可，你可以任选其一。
11	均衡器	jūn héng qì	equalizer	他调整了音响的均衡器，以改善音质。

 化知识【《三字经》】

　　《三字经》是中国传统启蒙读物之一，大多数学者认为其起源于宋代，由南宋学者王应麟所编写。其以三字一句的形式，文字简洁、押韵上口，可帮助儿童快速入门学习中华文化与传统道德。《三字经》全书约有一千字，主要内容包括四大类：教育与道德，强调学习的重要性；历史典故，简述中国的历史、介绍了重要的历史事件和人物；自然与社会知识，涉及天文、地理等；伦理与家庭观，强调孝道、忠诚、诚信等传统美德。

图 4-4　山东博物馆：孔子见老子画像石 "昔仲尼 师项橐"

　　在中国古代，几乎每个受过教育的儿童都会诵读《三字经》。此外，它不仅在中国影响深远，还通过文化传播，传到了韩国、日本、越南等国家，成为东亚文化圈中重要的经典教材之一。随着时代的发展，虽然现代教育体系发生了变化，但《三字经》仍然以其简洁明了的教育内容和丰富的文化内涵得到普遍认可，至今仍被广泛用于儿童的传统文化教育中。

　　今天，《三字经》不仅是一部启蒙读物，更是了解中华传统文化、伦理思想的重要桥梁。尽管有些内容在现代社会中需要被重新解释，但它所传递的孝顺、诚信、勤学等美德依然具有重要的现实意义。通过对《三字经》的学习，人们可以更好地了解和继承中华民族的优秀传统文化，提升自身的文化修养和道德素质。

治文物【《绍兴恤刑手诏碑》】

《绍兴恤刑手诏碑》现存于浙江绍兴一吟堂内，篆额"绍兴恤刑手诏"3行6字，碑文10行，行15字，诏书全文出自宋高宗赵构御书。末署御押，并于"九"字处钤"御书之宝"印。

图 4-5 《绍兴恤刑手诏碑》[1]

绍兴三年（1133 年），宋高宗赵构下诏："可布告中外，应为吾士师者，各务仁平，济以哀矜。天高听卑，福善祸淫，莫遂尔情，罚及尔身。置此座

---

〔1〕 参见《南宋·〈绍兴恤刑手诏碑〉》，载中国政法大学中华法制文明虚拟博物馆，https://flgj.cupl.edu.cn/info/1072/4194.htm，最后访问日期：2024 年 11 月 8 日。

右，永以为训。仍劄付台属宪臣，常加检察。"当年此诏首先刊立在临安都堂，随后以"墨本"（拓本）颁行郡县守令，命刻之庭石，置诸座右。碑文中的"廷尉"，秦汉时位列九卿，为中央最高司法审判机构长官，主管诏狱和修订律令等相关事宜；"士师"是古代对执法官员之通称。此诏文可见宋高宗重视国家法制体系建设、体恤民情的用心。

经 典阅读

《三字经》（节选）

人之初，性本善。性相近，习相远。
苟不教，性乃迁。教之道，贵以专。
昔孟母，择邻处。子不学，断机杼。
窦燕山，有义方。教五子，名俱扬。
养不教，父之过。教不严，师之惰。
子不学，非所宜。幼不学，老何为。
玉不琢，不成器。人不学，不知义。
为人子，方少时。亲师友，习礼仪。
香九龄，能温席。孝于亲，所当执。
融四岁，能让梨。弟于长，宜先知。
首孝弟，次见闻。知某数，识某文。
一而十，十而百。百而千，千而万。
三才者，天地人。三光者，日月星。
三纲者，君臣义。父子亲，夫妇顺。
曰春夏，曰秋冬。此四时，运不穷。
曰南北，曰西东。此四方，应乎中。
曰水火，木金土。此五行，本乎数。
曰仁义，礼智信。此五常，不容紊。

......

参考译文

人在刚出生的时候，本性都是善良的。本性彼此相近，但由于后天习惯，逐渐有了差异。

如果从小没有得到教育，本性就会发生变化。教育的方法，贵在专一。

从前孟子的母亲为了孩子的教育，选择了理想的邻居和居住环境。她看到孩子不认真学习，她就剪断了织机的布匹，以此教育孩子。

窦燕山教子有方，他教出了五个有成就的儿子，个个都很出名。

养育孩子却不教育，是父亲的过失；教育学生却不严格，是老师的懒惰。

孩子不学习，是不应该的。小时候不学习，长大后能做什么呢？

玉石如果不经过雕琢，就无法成为有用的器物；人如果不学习，就不能懂得道理。

作为子女，从小就应该亲近良师益友，学习礼节和道德。

黄香在九岁时就知道为父母暖被窝，对父母尽孝是每个孩子应该做到的。

孔融在四岁时就知道把大的梨子让给哥哥，尊敬和友爱兄长，这是从小就应该知道的道理。

做人首先要懂得孝顺父母、友爱兄弟，然后再学习各种知识。要学会认识数目，学习文字的含义。

数始于一，终于十。十个十累加为百，十个百累加为千，十个千累加为万，以至于无穷。

三才是指天地人，三光是指日月星。

三纲是指君臣、父子、夫妻的秩序。君臣有忠义，父子有亲情，夫妻有和顺。

春夏秋冬，是四个季节，循环往复没有穷尽。

南北西东，是四个方位，围绕中央。

水火木金土，是五行元素，来源于天数。

仁义礼智信，是五种美德，不可以混乱。

……

At the beginning, when people are born, their nature is good and pure. All human nature is similar, but habits make them different over time.

If not taught properly from childhood, one will have their nature changed. The way of teaching is valued by concentration.

In the past, Mencius' mother chose the ideal neighbourhood and living environment for her son's education. When her son did not study hard, she cut the fabric from her loom to teach him a lesson.

Dou Yanshan was a model father who was extremely skillful in educating his five sons, all of whom became successful and famous.

Raising a child without education is the father's fault. Lack of strictness in education is the laziness of teachers.

It is improper for children not to learn. If one doesn't learn in youth, what can they do when they grow up?

Jade that is not polished cannot become a useful object. A person who doesn't learn cannot understand morality.

As children, they should be close to good teachers and helpful friends, and learn etiquette and virtues from a young age.

At the age of nine, Huang Xiang knew to warm the bed for his parents. Being filial to parents is what every child should do.

At the age of four, Kong Rong knew to let his elder brothers have the bigger pears. Respecting older siblings is what every child should know.

First, we must know filial piety and brotherly love, then learn other knowledge. We must learn numbers and recognize words.

Numbers start from one and end at ten. Ten tens make a hundred. Ten hundreds make a thousand. Ten thousands makea ten thousand, and it can go on infinitely.

The "three forces" of the universe are Heaven, Earth, and People. The "three luminaries" are the Sun, Moon, and Stars.

The "three cardinal guides" refer to the order between sovereign and subject, father and son, husband and wife. There should be loyalty between ruler and minister, affection between father and son, and harmony between husband and wife.

Spring, summer, autumn, and winter are the four seasons, endlessly cycling.

South, north, west, and east are the four directions, centered around the middle.

Water, fire, wood, metal, and earth are the five elements, based on numbers.

Benevolence, righteousness, propriety, wisdom, and trustworthiness are the five virtues, which should never be disrupted.

…

课　后练习

1. 选择题：在宋朝，下列哪项措施不是对贼盗犯罪进行惩治的方法？

A. 加重对贼盗犯罪的法律处罚

B. 实施重法地特别法

C. 对所有民众一律加税

D. 通过编敕加强法律执行

2. 判断题：《盗贼重法》是宋朝特别针对某一地区制定并单独适用的刑事特别法，这种法律在中国古代是首次出现的。

3. 填空题：宋哲宗时期，《盗贼重法》覆盖的行政区划数达到＿＿＿＿个，表明宋朝对贼盗的惩罚范围非常广泛。

4. 简答题：描述宋朝对盗贼采用重法的后果，并简要说明它如何影响了社会秩序。

5. 讨论题：宋朝重典惩治贼盗的措施及其长期效果。请分析这些措施为什么未能有效解决盗贼问题，并讨论其对宋朝社会结构和法律体系的影响。

课　文参考翻译

In the middle period of the Northern Song Dynasty, faced with the rampant situation of thieves, the government took greater measures to punish such crimes by issuing a series of imperial decrees that intensified penalties for thieves. During the Jiayou period of Emperor Renzong of the Song Dynasty, the government declared harsher penalties for those caught stealing with a rod in the capital area, and in 1062, the "Harsh Law for Concealing Thieves" was introduced. This law designated the capital, Kaifeng, its counties, and four neighboring states as areas where anyone harboring thieves would face severe punishment. This set of laws, unique to specific regions and unprecedented in ancient China, resembled modern special criminal laws.

Under Emperor Yingzong, the scope of severe law areas was clarified to include extending harsh punishments such as family implication and property confiscation even for non- "Ten Abominations" robberies, which were not covered by Tang or Five Dynasties' laws.

Emperor Shenzong expanded the severe law areas established during Yingzong's reign with the "Harsh Law for Thieves," encouraging the public to denounce thieves and their harborers while increasing local officials' responsibilities in capturing thieves. This law was applied rigorously even outside the designated severe law areas.

By the time of Emperor Zhezong, the severe law areas included 17 of the 24 administrative regions of the Song Dynasty, with the "Harsh Law for Thieves" entirely replacing the "Criminal Code of Song Dynasty: Criminal Code on Theft" in these regions.

However, these exceptional legal measures, while intensifying punishments for theft and robbery, disrupted the standard legal order and adversely affected the penal system of the late feudal society. Despite these efforts, punitive deterrence did not eradicate banditry. On the contrary, theft and social disorder continued to increase. Consequently, in the late Northern Song period, Emperor Huizong implemented a dual strategy of military suppression and pacification through persuasion and amnesty.

During the Southern Song period, with increased social tensions, rulers intensified punishments against thieves. First-time offenders who avoided the death penalty were branded on the forehead with the word "强盗 brigand" as a mark of disgrace. Repeat offenders, including accomplices, were sentenced to death. But leniency was granted to criminals who were originally famine victims and forced to steal.

In summary, due to structural societal issues, theft remained a persistent problem throughout the Song Dynasty, leading to a consistent policy of harsh punishments for thieves until the Song Dynasty's end.

第五课

辽金元时期的法律（一）

课 前准备

图 5-1 内蒙古巴林左旗：祖州石室

公元 907 年，北方契丹族的耶律阿保机当选为契丹大首领，即可汗位。916 年，耶律阿保机自称皇帝，建立军事统治，后契丹国改称辽朝，定都上京（今内蒙古自治区赤峰市巴林左旗附近）。1125 年，辽朝被完颜阿骨打领导的金朝所灭。金是女真人建立的多民族国家，1115 年建国，国号大金，初期定都会宁（今黑龙江省哈尔滨市阿城区），后迁都中都（今北京市）。

辽、金两朝作为中国历史上重要的少数民族政权，其法律制度在继承和发展中原传统法律的基础上，结合自身的民族特点，形成了独特的法律体系。

辽、金时期，统治区域内多民族杂居，民族矛盾错综复杂，因此，辽、金时期制定的法律既带有鲜明的民族特色，又呈现出明显的汉化倾向。

In AD 907, the northern Khitan tribe, Yelu Abaoji, was elected as the great chief of the Khitan, that is, the khan. In 916, Yelu Abaoji proclaimed himself emperor and established military rule. Later, the state of Khitan was renamed the Liao Dynasty, with its capital at Shangjing (near present-day Balinzuoqi, Chifeng, Inner Mongolia). In 1125, Liao was destroyed by the Jin Dynasty under the leadership of Wanyan Aguda. Jin was a multi-ethnic state founded by the Jurchen people in 1115 under the name of Dajin, with its initial capital at Huining (present-day Acheng, Harbin, Heilongjiang) and later moved to Zhongdu (present-day Beijing).

The Liao and Jin Dynasties, as important ethnic minority regimes in Chinese history, formed a unique legal system based on the inheritance and development of traditional laws of the Central Plains, combined with their own ethnic characteristics.

During the Liao and Jin Dynasties, the ruling areas were inhabited by many ethnic groups and the ethnic conflicts were complicated, therefore, the laws of Liao and Jin had both distinctive ethnic characteristics and an obvious tendency of sinicization when making laws.

 生词表

序号	生词	词性	汉语拼音	英文解释
1	契丹	*proper n.*	Qì dān	Khitan, an ancient nomadic people in China
2	耶律阿保机	*proper n.*	Yē lǜ Ā bǎo jī	the founding emperor of the Liao Dynasty
3	军事统治	*phr.*	jūn shì tǒng zhì	military rule
4	上京	*proper n.*	Shàng jīng	the capital of the Liao Dynasty

续表

序号	生词	词性	汉语拼音	英文解释
5	巴林左旗	*proper n.*	Bā lín Zuǒ qí	a county-level administrative region
6	完颜阿骨打	*proper n.*	Wán yán Ā gǔ dǎ	the founding emperor of the Jin Dynasty
7	女真	*proper n.*	Nǚ zhēn	Jurchen, an ethnic minority in the northeastern region of ancient China
8	会宁	*proper n.*	Huì níng	the early capital of the Jin Dynasty
9	中都	*proper n.*	Zhōng dū	the capital of the Jin Dynasty
10	民族矛盾	*phr.*	mín zú máo dùn	national contradiction
11	杂居	*v.*	zá jū	reside in a mixed settlement, live together
12	汉化	*n.*	hàn huà	Sinicization

 读

　　辽朝早期的法律制度体现了"因俗而治"的特点，即根据不同民族的习俗来适用不同的法律。辽朝统治者在吸收中原封建正统法律思想的同时，保留并改造了本民族的传统习惯法，形成了独具特色的法律思想。金在进入中原以前也使用本民族的习惯法，后来随着统治区域的不断扩张，金逐步完成了封建化的进程，并编纂了成文法典。

 文

　　辽、金时期的法律思想与制度在中国历史上具有重要的地位和影响。这一时期的法律制度不仅继承了前代的法制传统，还融合了各民族的法律习惯，形成了独特的法律体系。

　　辽代法制最初对契丹人和汉人实行区别对待，体现了"因俗而治"的特

点。此后，辽代法律在发展过程中，不断吸收汉文化并受其他民族法律的影响，逐渐形成了具有多元特色的法制体系。辽代的法律体系，在一定程度上继承了契丹族的传统习惯法。契丹族在立国前，主要依靠习惯法来维持社会秩序。随着辽朝的建立，契丹族开始制定成文法，逐渐形成了较为系统的法律制度。辽太祖耶律阿保机令臣下"定律令"，制定《治契丹及诸夷之法》，将契丹诸游牧部族的习惯法进行统一编纂、整理，形成了这部契丹文法典。后辽兴宗重熙五年（1036年），参照唐代法制，制定颁布《重熙条制》，是当时的基本成文法典。

金是女真人建立的多民族国家，在建国初期，仍沿袭女真人旧制。后随着统治区域的不断扩展，逐步完成封建化的进程，在法制上出现辽、宋法律与金习惯法并存的局面。同时，金国也很注重法典的制定，金熙宗时期，编纂了金国的第一部成文法典——《皇统制》。

图 5-2　内蒙古巴林右旗：辽庆州白塔

生词表

序号	生词	词性	汉语拼音	英文解释
1	因俗而治	*phr.*	yīn sú ér zhì	governance according to customs
2	法律思想	*phr.*	fǎ lǜ sī xiǎng	legal thought
3	习惯法	*n.*	xí guàn fǎ	customary law
4	封建化	*n.*	fēng jiàn huà	feudalization
5	编纂	*v.*	biān zuǎn	compile，edit
6	成文法	*n.*	chéng wén fǎ	statutory law
7	法制传统	*phr.*	fǎ zhì chuán tǒng	legal tradition
8	汉文化	*proper n.*	Hàn wén huà	Han culture
9	诸夷	*phr.*	zhū yí	a general term for other border ethnic groups or tribes outside the Khitan in Liao Dynasty documents
10	重熙条制	*proper n.*	Chóng xī Tiáo zhì	the regulations promulgated during the Chongxi period of Emperor Xingzong of the Liao Dynasty
11	并存	*v.*	bìng cún	coexist
12	皇统制	*proper n.*	Huáng tǒng Zhì	the statutory law promulgated during the reign of Emperor Xizong of the Jin Dynasty

重 点汉字【捕】

　　捕，汉语一级字，本义为捕捉、捉拿，与人的行为动作紧密相关。该字在秦汉时期开始出现，初指捕捉逃亡罪犯，后泛指各种捕捉行为。捕字组合能力强，可组成"斩捕""捕杀"等词。现代汉语中，"捕"仍常用于描述捕捉行为，并引申出追寻、搜寻等含义，在司法实务和日常生活中均十分常见。

图 5-3　"捕"字篆刻（王琦 刻）

 汉字拓展

序号	词汇	汉语拼音	英文解释	例句
1	捕捉	bǔ zhuō	capture	他们在森林里捕捉到了一只野兔。
2	捕风捉影	bǔ fēng zhuō yǐng	make accusations on hearsay	他总是捕风捉影，造成不必要的误会。
3	捕猎	bǔ liè	hunting	古时候人们靠捕猎为生。
4	捕快	bǔ kuài	bailiff seizing criminals in a feudal yamen in the days of old	那个捕快非常机警，很难被蒙蔽。
5	捕杀	bǔ shā	catch and kill	为了保护村庄，他们捕杀了野狼。
6	捕头	bǔ tóu	head of the bailiffs	在那个小镇上，捕头是大家都尊敬的人。
7	捕获	bǔ huò	catch	他们在行动中捕获了几名逃犯。
8	猎捕	liè bǔ	hunt down	严禁非法猎捕野生动物。
9	捕食	bǔ shí	prey on	这种鸟类主要捕食昆虫。

化知识【关汉卿与《窦娥冤》】

关汉卿（约 1220 年~1300 年）是中国元代著名的杂剧作家，与马致远、白朴、郑光祖并称"元曲四大家"。作为元杂剧的开创者和代表人物，关汉卿的作品广泛反映社会生活，深刻揭露当时社会的不公和压迫。其作品以生动的戏剧对白、鲜明的人物塑造和强烈的社会批判精神著称，关汉卿也被后世尊为"曲圣"。

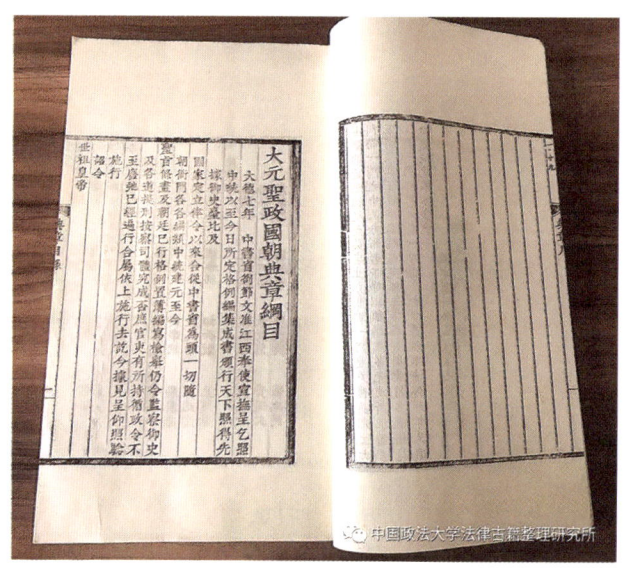

图 5-4　元·《元典章》[1]

《窦娥冤》是关汉卿最负盛名的代表作之一。主人公窦娥本是普通民间女子，幼年丧母，被卖给蔡婆婆为童养媳。丈夫早逝后，窦娥与蔡婆婆相依为命，却无辜卷入一场命案——当地恶徒张驴儿企图霸占窦娥，设计毒杀蔡婆婆，不料误杀其父亲。为逃脱罪责，张驴儿诬陷窦娥，而官府贪赃枉法，对

---

〔1〕 转引自《法制文物日历丨十月二十日·元·〈元典章〉》，载"中国政法大学法律古籍整理研究所"公众号 2019 年 10 月 20 日，https://mp.weixin.qq.com/s/RSPUINfP10bH_COV5b1-dQ，最后访问日期：2025 年 5 月 30 日。

窦娥严刑逼供。窦娥被逼承认莫须有的罪名，最终被判斩刑。临刑前，窦娥发下三桩誓愿：血溅白练而不落地、六月飞雪以证清白、楚州大旱三年以惩恶腐。窦娥被冤杀后，三桩誓愿一一应验，天地感应的奇迹使她的冤情昭然。窦娥的悲剧命运，既展现了底层女性的刚烈与无辜，也深刻揭露了元代社会的黑暗与腐败。

《窦娥冤》以其浓烈的悲剧力量和对社会现实的尖锐批判流传至今，不仅是元杂剧的巅峰之作，更是中国古典文学中叩问正义的永恒经典。关汉卿通过窦娥这一形象，持续叩击着人们内心对公正和正义的永恒追求。

法 治文物【《文昌阁祭田契券及佃约佃规碑》】

图 5-5 《文昌阁祭田契券及佃约佃规碑》[1]

《文昌阁祭田契券及佃约佃规碑》位于湖南省长沙市岳麓书院御书楼前右壁回廊，立笔于嘉庆二十二年（1817年）冬月上浣。碑呈长方形，纵80厘米，横188厘米。碑文共62行，由《文昌阁祭田契券》21行、《酌定祭田佃

---

[1] 参见《清·〈文昌阁祭田契券及佃约佃规碑〉》，载中国政法大学中华法制文明虚拟博物馆，https://flgj.cupl.edu.cn/info/1072/4926.htm，最后访问日期：2024年11月11日。

约稿》18 行、《公议祭田佃规租谷章程》9 行、《公议二月初三日祭祀条规》
13 行和立石年款及责任者 1 行组成。嘉庆二十二年（1817 年）冬月由岳麓书
院山长袁名曜勒石。

 典阅读

《窦娥冤》第三折（节选）

〔端正好〕没来由犯王法，不提防遭刑宪，叫声屈动地惊天！顷刻间游魂
先赴森罗殿，怎不将天地也生埋怨？

〔滚绣球〕有日月朝暮悬，有鬼神掌着生死权，天地也，只合把清浊分
辨，可怎生错看了盗跖颜渊？为善的受贫穷更命短，造恶的享富贵又寿延。
天地也，做得个怕硬欺软，却原来也这般顺水推船。地也，你不分好歹何为
地？天也，你错勘贤愚枉做天！哎，只落得两泪涟涟。

……

〔耍孩儿〕不是我窦娥罚下这等无头愿，委实的冤情不浅。若没些儿灵圣
与世人传，也不见得湛湛青天。我不要半星热血红尘洒，都只在八尺旗枪素
练悬，等他四下里皆瞧见。这就是咱苌弘化碧，望帝啼鹃。

……

〔二煞〕你道是暑气暄，不是那下雪天，岂不闻飞霜六月因邹衍？若果有
一腔怨气喷如火，定要感的六出冰花滚似绵，免着我尸骸现。要甚么素车白
马，断送出古陌荒阡！

……

〔一煞〕你道是天公不可期，人心不可怜，不知皇天也肯从人愿。做甚么
三年不见甘霖降？也只为东海曾经孝妇冤，如今轮到你山阳县。这都是官吏
每无心正法，使百姓有口难言！

……

〔煞尾〕浮云为我阴，悲风为我旋，三桩儿誓愿明题遍。婆婆也，直等待
雪飞六月，亢旱三年呵，那其间才把你个屈死的冤魂这窦娥显！

参考译文

〔端正好〕毫无理由地触犯王法，没想到会受到法律的惩罚，喊一声冤屈可以震天动地！转瞬之间，我的魂魄就被带到阴间，怎能不对天地生出怨恨呢？

〔滚绣球〕日月在天上日夜高悬，鬼神掌握着生死的权力，天地啊，你应该分辨清浊，为什么却错看了盗跖与颜渊？行善的人反而贫困命短，作恶的人却享富贵长寿。天地啊，你竟做出怕硬欺软的事，顺水推舟，原来也是这样！大地啊，你不分好坏如何称为大地？苍天啊，你错判贤愚，白做苍天！唉，只落得泪水涟涟。

〔耍孩儿〕不是我窦娥故意发下这无头的誓愿，实在是冤情深重。如果没有神灵来向世人证明，我就不会看到这明亮的天空。我不需要半滴热血洒在红尘中，只在那八尺长的白绫上悬挂，让所有人都能看到。正如苌弘化作碧血，望帝悲啼化作杜鹃。

〔二煞〕你以为这是暑热天气？难道不是下雪天吗？可曾听说过六月飞霜是因为邹衍的冤屈？如果真的有一腔冤屈如火般喷涌，就一定会感动天地，让六月飘雪，免得我曝尸荒野。何必需要什么素车白马，在这荒凉的古道送葬呢！

〔一煞〕你说老天不可预测，人心不可怜，但却不知道苍天也会依从人的愿望。为什么三年都不降甘霖？那是因为东海有孝妇的冤情，如今轮到你山阳县了。这都是官吏们没有良心不秉公执法，才使得百姓有口难言！

〔煞尾〕浮云为我遮阴，悲风为我旋绕，我的三桩誓愿全都明白昭告。婆婆啊，就等着六月飞雪，三年大旱吧，到那时才能替你这屈死的冤魂——窦娥昭雪！

〔端正好〕Without any reason, I violated the royal law, never expecting to be punished by law. A cry of injustice can rock the heavens and the earth! In an instant, my soul was taken to the underworld. How can I not harbor deep resentment against the heavens and the earth?

〔滚绣球〕The sun and moon shine aloft in the sky day and night, and the gods hold the power over life and death. Heaven and Earth, you should distinguish between purity and filth, but why did you mistake the wicked Zhi for the virtuous Yan Yuan? Those who do good end up poor and short-lived instead, while those who do evil enjoy wealth and long life. Heaven and Earth, even you fear the strong and bully the weak, just going with the current like this! Earth, if you can't tell right from wrong, how can you be called earth? Heaven, you wrongly judge the wise and the foolish—you are heaven in vain! Ah, I am left with nothing but endless tears.

〔耍孩儿〕It is not that I, Dou E, intentionally made such a groundless vow, But that my grievances run deeper than the sea. If no gods would bear witness to the world, I would never gaze upon this bright, unclouded sky. I want not a single drop of hot blood to stain the red dust—let it all hang upon an eight-foot white silk banner, that all may see. Like Chang Hong of the Zhou, whose blood turned to jade. Like King Wang of Shu, whose wails became the cuckoo's cry.

〔二煞〕Don't you think it's the heat of summer? And yet, isn't this a snowy day? Have you never heard how frost descended in June for Zou Yan, the unjustly wronged philosopher of Yan? If there burns a heart blazing with injustice like fire, it shall surely move heaven and earth to bring snow in June, sparing my body from lying unburied in the wild. Why need a funeral cart and white horse to lead me down this desolate path?

〔一煞〕You say heaven is unpredictable, heaven is unmerciful, yet you know not that heaven can also pity and fulfill human wishes. How is it that not a single drop of rain has fallen for three years? All because of a wronged and filial woman in Donghai—now disaster has come to Shanyang County. All this stems from officials who fail to uphold justice, leaving the people with grievances unheard!

〔煞尾〕Floating clouds obscure the sun for me, the mournful wind whirls around me—my three vows are now fully proclaimed. Mother, behold snow in June and three years of drought—only then will your wrongly slain soul—and mine, Dou E's—be vindicated!

 后练习

1. 选择题：辽、金时期的法律制度不仅继承了前代的法制传统，还融合了哪两者的法律习惯？

A. 各民族与契丹族

B. 各民族与汉文化

C. 契丹族与女真族

D. 汉文化与蒙古族

2. 判断题：金国在建国初期，就建立了新的法典。

3. 填空题：辽太祖耶律阿保机将契丹诸游牧部族的习惯法进行统一编纂、整理，形成了一部＿＿＿＿＿法典。

4. 简答题：辽代法制"因俗而治"的特点及其体现。

5. 讨论题：结合课文内容，分析辽代法律在发展过程中如何受汉文化和其他民族法律的影响而形成了具有多元特色的法制体系。

课　文参考翻译

The legal thought and system of the Liao and Jin Dynasties have an important position and influence in Chinese history. The legal system of this period not only inherited the legal tradition of the previous generation, but also integrated the legal customs of various ethnic groups to form a unique legal system.

The Liao legal system initially treated the Khitan and Han people differently, reflecting the characteristic of "governance according to customs." Thereafter, in the process of development, the Liao legal system absorbed the influence of Han culture and the laws of other ethnic groups, and gradually formed a legal system with diversified characteristics. The legal system of the Liao Dynasty inherited, to a certain extent, the traditional customary law of the Khitan people. Before the establishment of the Liao, the Khitan people mainly relied on customary law to maintain social order. With the establishment of the Liao, the Khitan began to formulate written laws and gradually developed a more systematic legal system. Emperor Taizu of the Liao Dynasty, Yelu Abaoji, ordered his ministers to "make laws and orders" and formulate the "Laws for Governing the Khitan and Various Ethnic Minorities," which unified and organized the customary laws of the nomadic tribes of the Khitan, forming a code of law in the Khitan language. Later, in the fifth year of the Chongxi reign (1036) of Emperor Xingzong of the Liao Dynasty, the "Chongxi Regulations" —enacted and promulgated with reference to the Tang Dynasty legal system—became the basic written code of that time.

Jin was a multi-ethnic state established by the Jurchen people, and in the early period of its establishment, it still followed the old system of the Jurchen people. With the continuous expansion of the ruling region, gradually complete the process of feudalization, the legal system in the Liao, Song law and Jin customary law coexist in the situation. At the same time, the Jin state also paid much attention to the formulation of the code during the reign of Emperor Xizong of the Jin Dynasty, compiled the first written code of Jin— "Huangtong Regulations".

第六课

辽金元时期的法律（二）

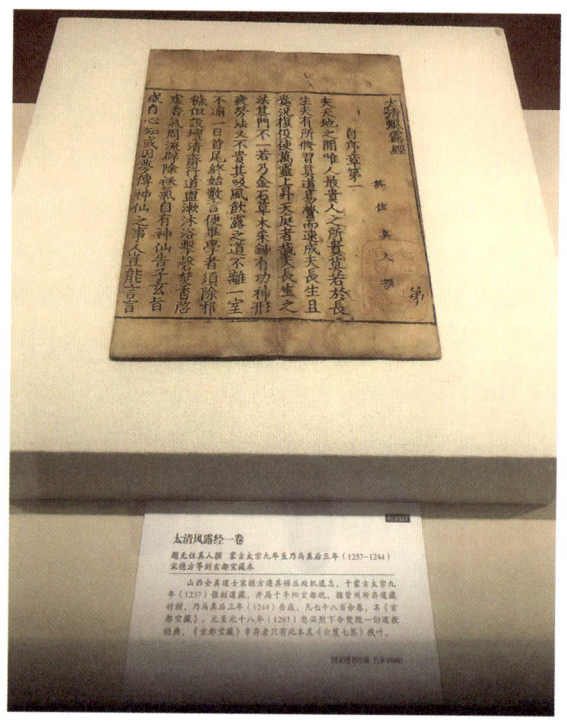
图 6-1 国家典籍博物馆：太清风露经一卷

13 世纪初，蒙古族各游牧部落结束内部纷争，在领袖铁木真的领导下实现统一，建立大蒙古国。铁木真被尊称为蒙古大汗——"成吉思汗"。1271 年，蒙古第五位大汗忽必烈建立元朝。元朝后期，政治腐败，民族矛盾与阶级矛盾日益加剧，导致爆发元末农民起义，元朝灭亡。元朝是以蒙古贵族为主体包括汉族地主阶级和其他各族上层共同建立的政权，其文化、制度呈现鲜明的多样性。[1]

〔1〕参见朱勇主编：《中国法律史》，中国政法大学出版社 2021 年版，第 228 页。

In the early 13th century, the various nomadic tribes of the Mongols ended their internal disputes and achieved unification under the leadership of the chieftain Temujin, who established the Great Mongol Empire. Temujin was honored as the Great Khan of the Mongols, known as "Genghis Khan." In 1271, Kublai Khan, the fifth Great Khan of the Mongols, founded the Yuan Dynasty. In the late period of the Yuan Dynasty, political corruption and the growing intensification of ethnic and class contradictions led to the outbreak of a large-scale peasant uprising, leading to its downfall. The Yuan Dynasty was a regime established primarily by Mongol nobles, including the Han landlord class and the upper echelons of various other ethnic groups. Its culture and institutions exhibited distinct diversity.

 生词表

序号	生词	词性	汉语拼音	英文解释
1	铁木真	*proper n.*	Tiě mù zhēn	an outstanding strategist and statesman in world history
2	蒙古大汗	*phr.*	měng gǔ dà hán	the common lord of all Mongols
3	忽必烈	*proper n.*	Hū bì liè	the founding emperor of the Yuan Dynasty
4	农民起义	*n.*	nóng mín qǐ yì	the uprising of peasants who have lost their land, generally reflecting the contradictions between the autocratic imperial court and the civil society

 读

　　元朝统治的区域以汉族聚居区为主，当地文化发展成熟，因此统治者在政权与法制建设中，参照了唐宋时期的制度，吸收了以儒家思想为核心的封建文明成果。同时，元朝在诸多方面延续了蒙古国原有的部分统治方式，保留了奴隶制及早期封建制的一些特征，如注重军事治理等。在社会治理中，元朝对不同族群采取了差异化的管理方式。根据早期研究观点，当时社会大致分为四个群体：蒙古人、色目人、汉人（包括元朝统一前已受蒙古统治的北方汉族及契丹、女真等族群）、南人（主要指原南宋统治区域的居民）。其中，蒙古人在社会管理中占据主导地位，而汉人群体，特别是南人，在社会结构中处于相对边缘的位置。[1]

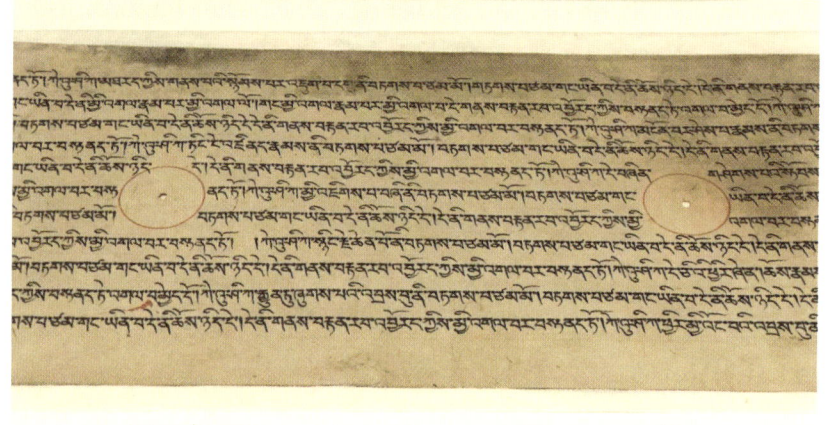

般若波罗蜜多十万颂

元抄本

图 6-2　国家典籍博物馆：《般若波罗蜜多十万颂》元抄本

在元朝，蒙古人在法律上享有特权。例如，汉人刑事案件由刑部系统管辖，而蒙古之案则由大宗正府管辖。在适用刑罚时同样因人而异：蒙古人因争执或趁酒醉打死汉人者，处以出征的刑罚，全额征收"烧埋银"（丧葬费）

---

〔1〕参见朱勇主编：《中国法律史》，中国政法大学出版社 2021 年版，第 229 页。

而不用偿命；反之，汉人打死蒙古人，照付烧埋银，仍要处死刑。蒙古人除犯死罪外，概不监禁，甚至不执拘，死刑犯被监禁时也不准拷掠。

元朝的法律确认蓄养奴婢的合法性。在蒙古政权的扩张过程中，存在"掠民为奴"的现象。元朝法律规定，奴隶属于"贱人"范畴，其身份被视为主人财产的一部分。在刑罚适用方面，元朝法律体现出主奴、良贱之间的差异。法律允许奴隶主对奴婢施行刺面、戴铁枷等刑罚。此外，若良人致贱人死亡，刑罚相对较轻，通常处以杖刑并赔偿烧埋银，无需承担死刑。

此外，元朝普遍尊崇佛教，"帝师"统领全国的佛教事务，并掌管藏族地区的政教事务，帝师的诏旨与皇帝的敕令具有同等的法律效力。僧侣可以以"布功德"为名，奏释重囚，僧侣除犯奸盗、诈伪、杀伤人命等重罪案件外，一般犯罪不受法律制裁；同时法律对一切侵害僧侣人身的行为予以严惩。[1]

 生词表

序号	生词	词性	汉语拼音	英文解释
1	色目	*proper n.*	Sè mù	a general term in the Yuan Dynasty for various ethnic groups in the northwest and western regions excluding the Mongols
2	刑部	*n.*	xíng bù	the official department in charge of criminal law and prison litigation affairs in China's feudal society
3	系统	*n.*	xì tǒng	system
4	管辖	*v.*	guǎn xiá	govern, administer
5	征收	*v.*	zhēng shōu	levy
6	烧埋银	*n.*	shāo mái yín	funeral expenses that muderers pay to the families of the victims
7	丧葬费	*n.*	sāng zàng fèi	funeral expenses
8	概不	*phr.*	gài bù	in no case

---

〔1〕　参见朱勇主编：《中国法律史》，中国政法大学出版社 2021 年版，第 232 页。

续表

序号	生词	词性	汉语拼音	英文解释
9	监禁	*v.*	jiān jìn	imprison
10	拷掠	*v.*	kǎo lüè	torture
11	刺面	*v.*	cì miàn	tattoo the face as a punishment
12	铁枷	*n.*	tiě jiā	iron necklock
13	帝师	*n.*	dì shī	the highest-ranking official in the Yuan Dynasty in charge of handing affairs related to Xizang and Buddhism
14	僧侣	*n.*	sēng lǚ	monk
15	奏释	*phr.*	zòu shì	submit a memorial to the throne to request the release of
16	侵害	*v.*	qīn hài	infringe，harm
17	严惩	*v.*	yán chéng	punish severely

重点汉字【证】

图 6-3 "证"字篆刻（王琦 刻）

证，汉语一级字，本义为告发，与人的行为动作紧密相关。该字的源头字形"證"在秦汉时期已经出现，其含义逐渐引申为通过证据来证明某事的真实性，进而泛指各种验证行为。"证"字组合能力强，可组成"证明""证实"

等词。现代汉语中，"证"仍常用于描述验证行为，并引申出确认、认证等含义，在司法实务和日常生活中均较为常见。

 汉字拓展

序号	词汇	汉语拼音	英文解释	例句
1	证明	zhèng míng	prove，demonstrate	他用这份文件来证明他的立场。
2	证据	zhèng jù	evidence	警察找到了他犯罪的证据。
3	证实	zhèng shí	confirm，verify	研究证实了这种药物的有效性。
4	证件	zhèng jiàn	document，credential	出国旅行时必须携带有效证件。
5	证券	zhèng quàn	security	他在股市上投资了多种证券。
6	证书	zhèng shū	certificate，diploma	他考取了职业资格证书。
7	凭证	píng zhèng	voucher，proof	我们需要一份交易凭证。
8	见证	jiàn zhèng	witness	他见证了公司的快速发展。
9	保证	bǎo zhèng	guarantee，ensure	我保证会按时完成工作。
10	合格证	hé gé zhèng	certificate of conformity	所有产品都必须有合格证才能出售。
11	身份证	shēn fèn zhèng	identity card	你去银行时不要忘记带身份证。
12	诊断证明	zhěn duàn zhèng míng	diagnostic certificate	医生为他出具了一份诊断证明。
13	认证	rèn zhèng	authenticate	该机构专门负责产品质量认证。
14	驾驶证	jià shǐ zhèng	driver's license	他刚刚取得了驾驶证。

 化知识【赵孟頫与《鹊华秋色图》】

赵孟頫（1254年~1322年）是中国元代著名的书画家、文学家和书法家，是元代初期重要的文化人物之一。赵孟頫出身宋朝皇族，祖先是宋太祖赵匡胤，因此他身上带有浓厚的宋代文化底蕴。宋朝灭亡后，赵孟頫致仕于元廷，成为元代宫廷的重要官员。他在书法、绘画、文学等方面都有着卓越的成就，尤其在书法和绘画方面具有极高的影响力，被称为"元人冠冕"。

赵孟頫的书法深受"二王"（王羲之、王献之）风格的影响，讲究笔法的流畅与变化。他以复古创新的态度，成功地融合了宋代文人画的精神与元代的艺术风格。他的画作兼具文人气息和高超的艺术技巧，追求笔墨的精妙和意境的表达，作品中蕴含着丰富的诗意与哲思。

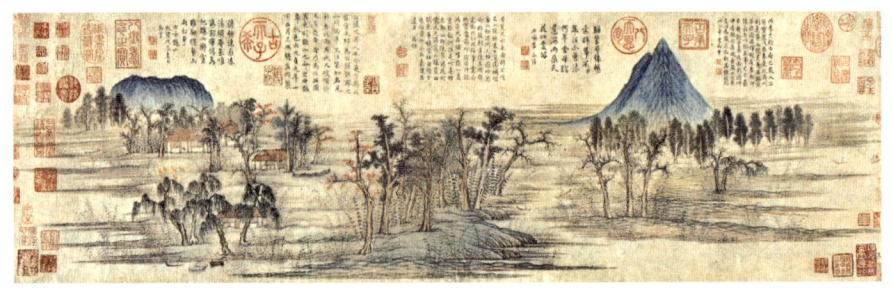

图 6-4　元·《鹊华秋色图》（赵孟頫）

赵孟頫的代表作之一是浅绛山水《鹊华秋色图》。该画作创作于 1295 年，描绘了济南鹊山和华不注山的秋日景色。这幅画卷以水墨渲染，笔法洗练，富有诗意地表现了秋天山水的清幽与雅致。在这幅画中体现了赵孟頫对传统山水画的继承与创新，即将宋代山水画的精致与元代的文人画风相结合。

在《鹊华秋色图》中，赵孟頫用清淡的墨色表现了山川的起伏和秋日的宁静，画中的山峦、林木、河流以及渔船等景物层次分明，显得既简洁又细腻，呈现出一种宁静悠远的意境。这幅画的特别之处在于，它并没有追求大气磅礴的构图，而是用精巧的布局和流畅的笔墨表达出山水的静谧之美，给人一种亲切自然的感觉。其柔和的线条和流畅的笔墨传递了艺术家对自然景物的深刻观察与理解，展示了元代初期文人画家对自然景观的细腻体会和悠然情怀。这幅画中，赵孟頫所表现的山水清新、淡雅，有着悠远的意境，充分反映了他对自然的热爱和对生活的恬淡态度。赵孟頫善于将山水与人文情感相结合，使得画作充满了浓厚的文人气息。

作为元代文人画家的代表人物之一，赵孟頫的《鹊华秋色图》不仅展现了他高超的艺术技巧，还深刻地表达了他对传统文化的敬仰和对艺术创作的独特理解。这幅画被后人视为中国山水画的经典之一，也标志着元代山水画在表现手法和精神内涵上的重要发展。赵孟頫通过《鹊华秋色图》传递出一种宁静、和谐的美感，成为后世许多画家学习和模仿的对象，对中国绘画艺术的发展产生了深远的影响。

法 治文物【《文昌帝君圣像阴骘文碑》】

图 6-5　《文昌帝君圣像阴骘文碑》[1]

此碑立于上海市汇龙潭公园文昌阁。

碑上部横题"文昌帝君圣像阴骘文"，碑身上半绘图，下半刻文 25 行，满行 32 字，首行为"文昌帝君阴骘文"，时铭书，裴大令、裴奉尧刊。碑文

---

〔1〕　参见《清·〈文昌帝君圣像阴骘文碑〉》，载中国政法大学中华法制文明虚拟博物馆，https://flgj.cupl.edu.cn/info/1072/4893.htm，最后访问日期：2024 年 11 月 21 日。

《文昌帝君阴骘文》一般认为成书于元代，是道教三大劝善书之一，主要劝导人们广行阴骘（阴德），做善事。全文教人止恶修善，不仅在行为上要断恶修善，更要在心地上规范自己。

《增广贤文》（节选）

昔时贤文，诲汝谆谆。集韵增广，多见多闻。观今宜鉴古，无古不成今。知己知彼，将心比心。酒逢知己饮，诗向会人吟。相识满天下，知心能几人。相逢好似初相识，到老终无怨恨心。近水知鱼性，近山识鸟音。易涨易退山溪水，易反易覆小人心。运去金成铁，时来铁似金。读书须用意，一字值千金。逢人且说三分话，未可全抛一片心。

 参考译文

过去的圣贤所留下的文章，会谆谆教诲着你。这些文章被汇编为《增广贤文》，让你能够增长见闻、开阔视野。观察现今的社会，应当借鉴古代的经验，因为没有古代的历史积累，就没有今天的成就。了解自己也要了解对方，要设身处地为他人着想。遇到知己时，才值得与他一同饮酒；遇到懂诗的人，才值得与他一起吟诗。虽然认识的人遍布天下，但真正知心的人又有几个呢？与人相处时保持像初次见面的客气与礼貌，那么即使到了老年，也不会产生怨恨之心。接近水边，才能了解鱼的习性；靠近山林，才能识别鸟儿的叫声。山间的溪水容易涨也容易退，小人的心思则容易反复无常。运气不好的时候，金子也会变成铁；时来运转的时候，铁也会变得像金子一样珍贵。读书时需要用心思考，因为每一个字都蕴含着千金的价值。与人交往时，说话要留有余地，不可轻易把内心的想法完全透露给别人。

The wise words of the past earnestly instruct you. These writings, compiled into *Zengguang Xianwen*, broaden your knowledge and expand your horizons. Observing the present should be done with reference to the past, as there is no present without the past. Knowing oneself and understanding others, empathizing with others. Drink wine with a confidant, recite poetry with someone who appreciates it. Although you may know many people, how many people truly understand you? Be polite when getting along with people as you meet for the first time, so that even in old age, there will be no resentment. Being close to water, you understand the nature of fish; being near mountains, you recognize the sounds of birds. Mountain streams rise and fall easily, just as the hearts of petty people are fickle. When luck is gone, gold turns to iron; when fortune comes, iron becomes like gold. Reading requires effort, as each word is worth a fortune. When interacting with others, speak cautiously and do not reveal all your thoughts.

课 后练习

1. 选择题：元朝时期，汉人刑事案件由哪个部门管辖？

A. 大宗正府

B. 刑部系统

C. 国师府

D. 帝师府

2. 判断题：元朝的法律确认了蓄养奴婢的合法性。

3. 填空题：在元朝，蒙古人除犯死罪，概不监禁，甚至不执拘，死罪监禁也不准_____。

4. 简答题：元朝有罪的蒙古人和汉人在刑罚适用上的差异。

5. 讨论题：结合元朝的法律制度，分析其对蒙古人赋予的法律特权及其社会影响。

课 文参考翻译

During the Yuan Dynasty, Mongolians enjoyed legal privileges. For instance, criminal cases involving Han people were governed by the Ministry of Punishment, while cases involving Mongols people were handled by the Office of the Imperial Clan Affairs. The application of penalties also varied depending on the person involved. If a Mongol killed a Han person due to a dispute or while drunk, the punishment was conscription and a fine for burial expenses, without death punishment. Conversely, if a Han person killed a Mongol, the punishment was death and a fine for burial expenses. Mongols, except for those committing capital crimes, were generally not imprisoned or even detained. Even for capital crimes, they were not subjected to torture.

The laws of the Yuan Dynasty confirmed the legality of keeping slaves.During the expansion of the Mongol regime, there was a phenomenon of "capturing people as slaves." According to the laws of the Yuan Dynasty, slaves were classified into the category of "贱人" (inferior persons) and their status was regarded as part of their masters' property. In terms of the application of penalties, the law reflected differences between masters and slaves, as well as between "良人" (commoners) and inferior persons. The law permitted slave owners to impose punishments such as tattooing the face and putting on iron shackles on slaves. Additionally, if a commoner caused the death of a inferior person, the penalty was relatively light, usually consisting of flogging and compensation for funeral expenses, without the need to bear the death penalty.

In addition, the Yuan Dynasty widely revered Buddhism. The Imperial Preceptor oversaw Buddhism nationwide and managed the political and religious affairs of the Xizang regions. The edicts of the Imperial Preceptor had the same legal effect as the emperor's decrees. Monks could petition for the release of serious prisoners in the name of "merit-making." Monks were generally exempt from legal punishment, except in cases of serious crimes such as adultery, theft, fraud, and murder. However, the law severely punished any acts that harmed monks.

第七课

明朝时期的法律（一）

课 前准备

公元1368年，明太祖朱元璋在南京称帝，开始了明王朝的统治。朱元璋出身寒微，在取得政权后，十分注意总结前朝治理国家的经验教训。他的立法思想指导了明初的立法实践。在法律制度方面，明朝继承唐宋律的基本内容，在法律结构、立法技术等方面又有进一步发展。

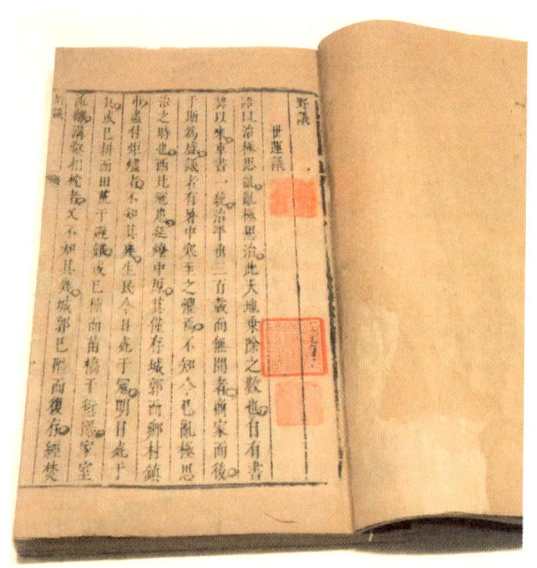

图7-1　江西省图书馆：明·《宋应星四种》明崇祯刻本

朱元璋总结元朝灭亡的历史教训，认为元败于"纵弛"，因而主张重典治国。与前代相比，明朝法律加重了对谋反、谋大逆等罪的处罚，扩大了株连的范围，严厉打击贼盗以及官吏贪赃枉法等罪行，这都是重典治国的体现。《明史》记载：*"明太祖惩元季吏治纵弛，民生凋敝，重绳贪吏，置之严典。"*朱元璋亲定的《明大诰》，尤其体现了重治贪官的思想。不过，礼法结合、德主刑辅是中国古代治理国家的信条，即便如朱元璋这样喜用重典的统治者，也主张明刑弼教。他认为刑罚的手段不过是为了挽救时弊，要达到国家的治理还必须用教化的方法。因此朱元璋在重视法律作用的同时强调*"法贵简当，*

使人易晓"，即法律应当简洁明了，容易使人知晓。[1]

In 1368, Zhu Yuanzhang, Emperor Taizu of the Ming Dynasty, proclaimed himself emperor in Nanjing, beginning the reign of the Ming Dynasty. Zhu Yuanzhang came from a humble background. After he gained power, he paid great attention to summing up the experience and lessons of the previous dynasties in governing the country. His legislative thought guided the legislative practice in the early Ming Dynasty. In the aspect of legal system, the Ming Dynasty inherited the basic content of the legal systems of Tang and Song Dynasties, and made further progress in legal structure and legislative technology.

Zhu Yuanzhang summed up the historical lessons of the collapse of the Yuan Dynasty, and believed that the Yuan was defeated by "laxity" , so he advocated governing the country with strict laws. Compared with the previous dynasties, the laws of the Ming Dynasty imposed heavier penalties on crimes such as treason and high treason, expanded the scope of collateral punishment, and severely cracked down on crimes such as thieves and officials taking bribes and bending the law, which were the embodiment of governing the country with severe laws. *The History of the Ming Dynasty* said, "The Emperor Taizu of the Ming Dynasty, in response to the lax governance of officials and the miserable livelihood of the people as well as the economic decline in the late Yuan Dynasty, severely punished corrupt officials and imposed strict laws on them." "Great Admonition of Ming Dynasty," written by Zhu Yuanzhang personally, especially embodies the thought of severely punishing corrupt officials. However, the combination of etiquette and law,along with the principle of 'morality-primary and punishment-auxiliary,' were the creeds of the ancient Chinese governance of the state, even an emperor like Zhu

---

〔1〕 参见朱勇主编：《中国法律史》，中国政法大学出版社 2021 年版，第 240~242 页。

Yuanzhang, who liked to use heavy rules, also advocated enlightening people through punishment. He believed that the means of punishment was only to save the current problems, and to achieve the governance of the country must also use the method of education. Zhu Yuanzhang not only attached importance to the role of law, but also emphasized that "the law should be simple and adequate, so that people are easy to understand," that is, the law should be concise and easy to make people know.

 生词表

序号	生词	词性	汉语拼音	英文解释
1	纵弛	*v.*	zòng chí	be lax and indulgent in governing
2	重典	*n.*	zhòng diǎn	harsh legal measures
3	谋反	*n.*	móu fǎn	the plotting of a rebellion
4	谋大逆	*n.*	móu dà nì	the plotting of great treason
5	贪赃枉法	*idm.*	tān zāng wǎng fǎ	embezzlement and perversion of law
6	重绳	*v.*	zhòng shéng	severely punish
7	严典	*n.*	yán diǎn	strict rules
8	礼法	*n.*	lǐ fǎ	rites and laws
9	时弊	*n.*	shí bì	current malpractices
10	简当	*adj.*	jiǎn dāng	simple and appropriate
11	易晓	*adj.*	yì xiǎo	easy to understand

 导 读

　　明朝继承并发展了唐宋时期的立法成就，其法律体系更趋完善，法律内容更加丰富。明朝的法律形式主要有律、令、诰、例、典等，其中律是主要

的法律形式，其他形式是律的补充。但在司法实践中，其他法律形式也分别发挥着相当重要的作用。在明朝修订和创制的一系列法律法规中，《大明律》、《明大诰》、《问刑条例》和《大明会典》代表了明朝法律的最高成就。

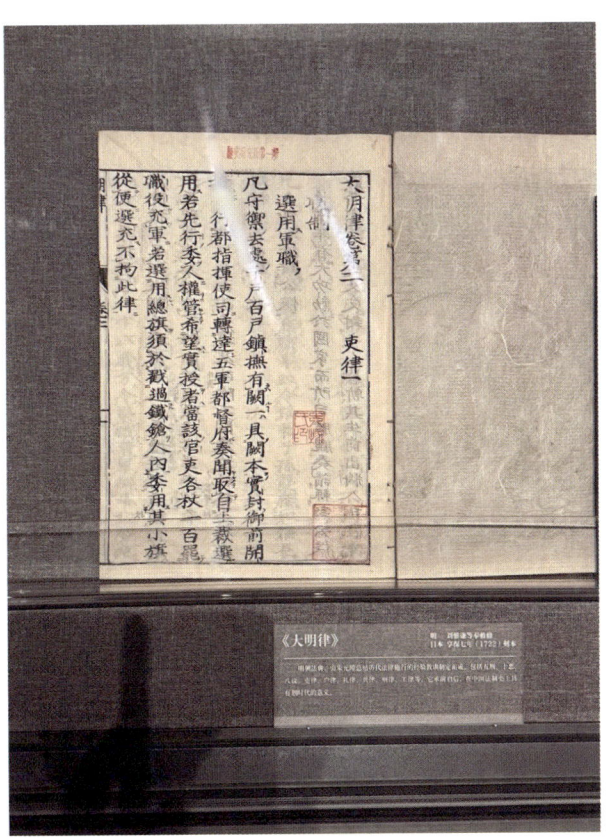

图 7-2　中国考古博物馆：《大明律》

　　《大明律》是明朝的基本法典。根据《明史·刑法志》的记载，《大明律》的制定颁行，经历了四个阶段，即**"草创于吴元年，更定于洪武六年，整齐于二十二年，至三十年始颁示天下"**。洪武三十年（1397 年），《大明律》历经30 年的更定和修改，最终完成并颁行全国，成为明朝的一代大法。明太祖对这部法律倾注了心血，曾下诏**"令子孙守之。*群臣有稍议更改，即坐以变乱祖制之罪。*"** 因此，《大明律》经这次正式颁行以后，继任的明朝诸位帝王都没有再对律文内容进行过修改。《大明律》全律共分 7 篇、30 卷、460 条，以《名例律》作为首篇，然后按吏、户、礼、兵、刑、工六部的国家机关分工编目，改变了以往法典分立篇目的原则和传统，是我国古代立法制度史上的一大变化，同时也体现了明太祖在官制改革中废除宰相制后，利用立法手段强化君主专制和中央集权的意图。在制定《大明律》期间，朱元璋鉴于彼时徇私废公、违法犯罪行为越来越多，又先后制定了《御制大诰》、《御制大诰续编》、《御制大诰三编》和《大诰武臣》等四编《明大诰》，共有 236 个条目，目的是使臣民**"*使知趋吉避凶之道*"**。《明大诰》的主要内容是惩治贪赃官吏和害民豪强，最大的特点是法外用刑，其中规定的刑罚如族诛、凌迟、挑筋、去指等体现了《明大诰》的残酷性。

 生词表

序号	生词	词性	汉语拼音	英文解释
1	制定	*v.*	zhì dìng	formulate，establish
2	草创	*v.*	cǎo chuàng	initiate，start from scratch
3	更定	*v.*	gēng dìng	revise，amend
4	整齐	*v.*	zhěng qí	systematize，regulate
5	颁示	*v.*	bān shì	promulgate，announce
6	倾注	*v.*	qīng zhù	pour into，devote
7	变乱	*v.*	biàn luàn	alter and disrupt
8	祖制	*n.*	zǔ zhì	ancestral system
9	徇私废公	*idm.*	xùn sī fèi gōng	act in self-interest and neglect public duties
10	御制	*adj.*	yù zhì	made by the emperor
11	续编	*v.*	xù biān	continue to compile，additional compilation
12	豪强	*n.*	háo qiáng	local tyrant，bully
13	族诛	*n.*	zú zhū	extermination of a family or clan for a crime

续表

序号	生词	词性	汉语拼音	英文解释
14	凌迟	*n.*	líng chí	slow slicing，death by a thousand cuts
15	挑筋	*n.*	tiāo jīn	tendon severing
16	去指	*n.*	qù zhǐ	amputation of fingers

重 点汉字【赦】

图 7-3 "赦"字篆刻（王琦刻）

赦，汉语一级字，其本义为宽免罪过。例如："掌三刺三宥三赦之法"——《周礼·秋官司刺》；"赦止者免止之罪辞也"——《公羊传·昭公》；"臣从其计，大王亦幸赦臣"——《史记·廉颇蔺相如列传》。赦也有"宽容"之意，如"先有司，赦小过，举贤才"——《论语·子路》。

 汉字拓展

序号	词汇	汉语拼音	英文解释	例句
1	赦书	shè shū	edict of pardon	皇帝的赦书宣布后，他重获了自由。
2	赦命	shè mìng	imperial pardon	接到赦命，他喜极而泣。
3	赦宥	shè yòu	pardon，clemency	皇帝将赦宥他们。
4	赦恕	shè shù	forgive，pardon	他祈求神明赦恕他的罪过。

续表

序号	词汇	汉语拼音	英文解释	例句
5	赦过	shè guò	pardon offenses	念在他是初犯，公司决定赦过。
6	大赦天下	dà shè tiān xià	general amnesty	今虽大赦天下，独不赦此四人。
7	赦放	shè fàng	pardon and release	国王决定赦放此囚。
8	罪在不赦	zuì zài bù shè	unforgivable	他犯下如此罪行，显然罪在不赦。
9	十恶不赦	shí è bù shè	unpardonable	他犯下的并不是十恶不赦的罪过。

文 化知识【《永乐大典》——"世界有史以来最大的百科全书"】

　　明朝永乐年间，明成祖朱棣命解缙、姚广孝等文臣主持编纂了一部集中国古代典籍于大成的类书，宗旨是"凡书契以来经史、子集、百家之书，至于天文、地志、阴阳、医卜、僧道、技艺之言，备辑为一书"。全书于永乐五年（1407年）定稿，一共 22 877 卷，11 095 册，约 3.7 亿字，汇集了古今图书七八千种，明成祖亲自撰写序言并赐名《永乐大典》。

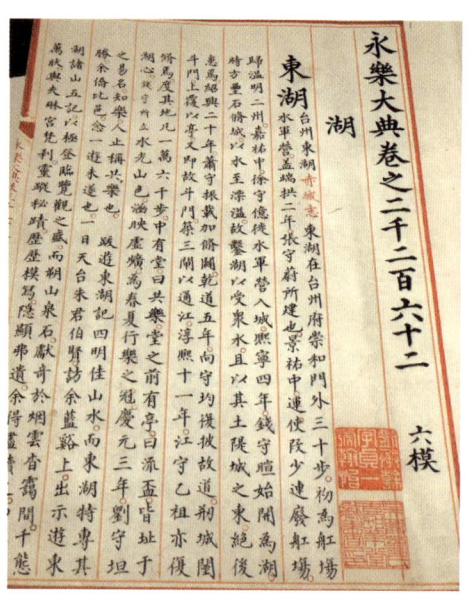

图 7-4　国家典籍博物馆：明·《永乐大典》

《永乐大典》内容包括经、史、子、集，涉及天文地理、阴阳医术、占卜、佛教、道教、戏剧、工艺、农艺等，涵盖了中华民族数千年来的知识财富。《不列颠百科全书》在"百科全书"条目中称中国明代类书《永乐大典》为"世界有史以来最大的百科全书"，《永乐大典》已经成为中国文化的一个重要符号。遗憾的是，《永乐大典》正本已经散佚不见，副本也大多毁于火灾和战乱，还有相当一部分被后人以修书之名窃走，现今仅存 800 余卷且散落于世界各地。

法 治文物【《赡学田颂碑》】

图 7-5　《赡学田颂碑》[1]

---

〔1〕 参见《明·〈赡学田颂碑〉》，载中国政法大学中华法制文明虚拟博物馆，https://flgj.cupl.edu.cn/info/1072/4359.htm，最后访问日期：2024 年 11 月 25 日。

此碑立于陕西省西安碑林博物馆。碑高 252 厘米，宽 61 厘米，厚 16 厘米。螭首方趺，额篆"大明西安赡学田颂" 2 行 8 字。碑身 10 行，满行 25 字。碑文系赞扬明太祖朱元璋下令让全国各郡县的学校重新修建祭祀先代圣人、先代贤师的庙宇，并且扩充增加学校的田产以作办学经费，以致"郡县庙祀绝复兴，礼修乐备昭圣明"之功绩。

经 典阅读

《从政录》第一章（节选）[1]

孔子曰："不患无位，患所以立。"惟亲历者知其味。余忝清要，日夜思念，于职事万无一尽，况敢恣肆于礼法之外乎？

程子书"视民如伤"四字于座侧，余每欲责人，尝念此意而不敢忽。

凡国家礼文制度法律条例之类，皆能熟视而深考之，则有以酬应世务而合乎时宜。

作官者于愚夫愚妇，皆当敬以临之，不可忽也。

学者大病在行不著，习不察，故事理不能合一。处事即求合一，处事即求合理，则行著习察矣。

处事最当熟思缓处。熟思则得其情，缓处则得其当。

一字不可轻与人，一言不可轻许人，一笑不可轻假人。

至诚以感人，犹有不服，况设诈以行之乎？

防小人密于自修。

事最不可轻忽，虽至微至易者，皆当以慎重处之。

丙吉深厚不伐，张安世谨慎周密，皆可为人臣之法。

论万事皆当以三纲五常为本。学者之所讲明践履，仕者之所表倡推明，皆当以三纲五常为本。舍此则学非所学，仕非所仕也。

---

〔1〕《从政录》是明代一部语录体著作，记录了作者的从政感悟。作者薛瑄（1389 年~1464 年），字德温，号敬轩。河东河津（今山西省运城市）人。明代著名思想家、理学家、文学家，河东学派的创始人，世称"薛河东"。薛瑄为官执法如山，正气凛然，其在《从政录》中概括了清官的三种类型，并探讨了重典治吏的深层原因。

按物太宜含弘，如行旷野，而有展布之地，不然太狭，而无以自容矣。

左右之言不可轻信，必审是实。

为政通下情为急。

 参考译文

孔子说："不怕没有职位，而怕没有立身之本。"只有亲身经历的人才知道其中的滋味。我虽然身居要职，但日夜思考，对于职责没有一事做到尽善尽美，又怎敢在礼法之外任性妄为呢？

程子在座位旁写下"视民如伤"四个字，每当我想要责备别人时，常常想起这句话，就不敢轻忽了。

凡是国家的礼仪、文化、制度、法律、法规等，都应该仔细研究和深思熟虑，这样才能应对世间事务，并合乎时宜。

作为官员面对普通百姓，都应该恭敬以待，不可轻视。

学者最大的弊病在于做事却不明白其中的道理，习惯了某些行为却不去仔细省察，因此事理不能合一。处理事情应该追求事理统一，这样行为才会符合道理，那么就能做到做事情明白道理，对习惯行为仔细省察了。

处理事情最应该深思熟虑，从容处理。深思熟虑则能洞察事情的真相，从容处理则能做到恰到好处。

一字不可轻易给人，一言不可轻易答应人，一笑不可轻易表露给人。

以最诚挚的情意来感动别人，尚且有人不被感动，何况是用诡计来行事呢？

要防备小人，就需密切注意自我修养。

处理事情不可马虎，即使是非常微小和简单的事情，也应当谨慎对待。

丙吉为人深厚宽厚，从不夸耀自己，张安世为人谨慎周密，他们都可以作为臣子的榜样。

讨论世间所有事情都应以三纲五常为根本。学者的讲解和实践，官员的倡导和推广，都应以三纲五常为根本。若舍弃了这些，那么做学问就不是真正的做学问，做官也不是真正的在履行官职的职责。

处理事物应当包容广泛，如行走在广阔的野外，有足够的空间来展开，否则太过狭窄，将没有容身之地。

不可轻信身边人的话，必须审查其真实性。

做政治的急务是了解下层民众的情况。

Confucius said, "One should not worry about not having a position, but rather about lacking the foundation to establish oneself." Only those who have experienced it can understand its essence. Although I hold an important office, I think day and night about my duties, and there is not a single task that I have accomplished perfectly. How then could I dare to act recklessly outside the norms of propriety?

Cheng Yi inscribed the words "Treat the people as if they are patients" beside his seat. Whenever I want to reprimand someone, I recall these words and dare not act rashly.

All national rites, cultural norms, systems, laws, and regulations should be carefully studied and deeply contemplated, so as to respond to worldly affairs and be appropriate for the times.

As an official, one should treat every ordinary people with respect and should never look down upon them.

The greatest drawback for scholars lies in the fact that they do things without understanding the underlying principles, and they get accustomed to certain behaviors without carefully examining them. Hence their inability to integrate principles with practice. In dealing with matters, one should strive for the unity of principles and affairs. Only in this way will one's actions conform to the principles, and then one can both understand the principles while doing things and carefully examine one's habitual behaviors.

When handling affairs, one should think deeply, act slowly and handle them calmly. Thinking deeply enables one to grasp the situation accurately, and handling it calmly enables one to act appropriately.

One should not lightly give away a word, promise anything casually, or grant a smile without due consideration.

Even when using the most sincere feelings to move others, there are still those who won't be touched. How much less so with deception?

Guard against petty people by closely monitoring one's own conduct.

Even the smallest and simplest matters should not be taken with utmost care.

Bing Ji, who is profound without boasting, and Zhang Anshi, who is careful and meticulous, both can serve as models for ministers.

In discussing all matters in the world, the principles of the Three Cardinal Guides and the Five Constant Virtues should be the foundation. Both scholars in their teachings and officials in their governance should base their actions on these principles. Without these, one's learning is not true learning, and one's service is not true service.

When handling matters, one should embrace a broad perspective, akin to walking in an open field where there is ample space to unfold. Otherwise, if too constrained, one will find no room to maneuver.

One should not readily believe the words of those around; it is essential to verify their truthfulness.

In governance, a priority is to understand the situation of the lower classes.

课 后练习

1. 选择题：明太祖朱元璋总结元朝灭亡的历史教训，认为元败于"纵弛"，因而主张采取的治国原则是_____。

A. 严格法纪

B. 效法唐律

C. 文官治国

D. 重典治国

2. 判断题：《大明会典》是明朝最基本的法律。

3. 填空题：在明朝修订和创制的一系列法律法规中，_____、《大诰》、_____和《大明会典》，代表了明朝法律的最高成就。

4. 简答题：《大明律》相较以往法典在体例上有什么重要变化？

5. 讨论题：明朝的行政、立法、司法和军事等权力均集中于皇帝一人之手，请思考明朝的统治者都采取了哪些制度来实现权力的高度集中。这些制度产生了哪些消极影响？

课 文参考翻译

"Statutes of Great Ming Dynasty" was the fundamental legal code of the Ming Dynasty. According to *The History of the Ming Dynasty: Records of Penal Law*, the creation and promulgation of the "Statutes of Great Ming Dynasty" underwent four stages: "Initiated in the first year of Wu era, revised in the sixth year of Hongwu, refined in the twenty-second year of Hongwu era, and finally promulgated throughout the empire in the thirtieth year of Hongwu era." In the thirtieth year of the Hongwu era（1397）, after thirty years of revisions and modifications, the "Statutes of Great Ming Dynasty" was completed and implemented nationwide, becoming the grand law of the Ming era. The Ming Dynasty's founder, Emperor Hongwu, devoted great efforts to this code and decreed "Order the descendants to abide by it. If any minister attempts to make changes, he will be charged with the crime of disrupting the ancestral system." Therefore, after its official enactment, subsequent Ming emperors made no further modifications to the content of the law. The "Statutes of Great Ming Dynasty" consists of 7 sections, 30 volumes, and 460 articles, with the "Names and Examples" as the opening section. The code was organized according to the division of labor of the six Ministries—Personnel, Revenue, Rites, War, Punishments, and Works—changing the traditional principle of the separate sections in legal codes. This represented a major shift in the legislative system history of ancient China and also reflected Emperor Hongwu's intent to strengthen the centralized autocratic rule through legislative means after abolishing the chancellor system. During the drafting of the "Statutes of Great

Ming Dynasty," seeing the increase in acts of corruption and criminal offenses, Zhu Yuanzhang also formulated the "Imperial Edict of Great Admonitions," "Sequel to Imperial Edict of Great Admonitions," "Third Compilation of Imperial Edict of Great Admonitions," and "Great Admonitions for Military Officials" in four parts, totaling 236 articles, aimed at instructing the subjects on how to "embrace good fortune and avoid disaster." The main content of the "Great Admonitions of Ming Dynasty" focused on punishing corrupt officials and harmful local magnates, with a notable feature being the application of extrajudicial punishments, including penalties such as extermination of clans, death by dismemberment, and removal of tendons or fingers, reflecting the severe nature of the decrees.

第八课

明朝时期的法律（二）

前准备

　　明朝行政、立法、司法和军事等权力高度集中于皇帝一人之手，中国古代的君主专制进一步加强，但这也导致了明朝的政治腐败至明朝后期愈演愈烈。

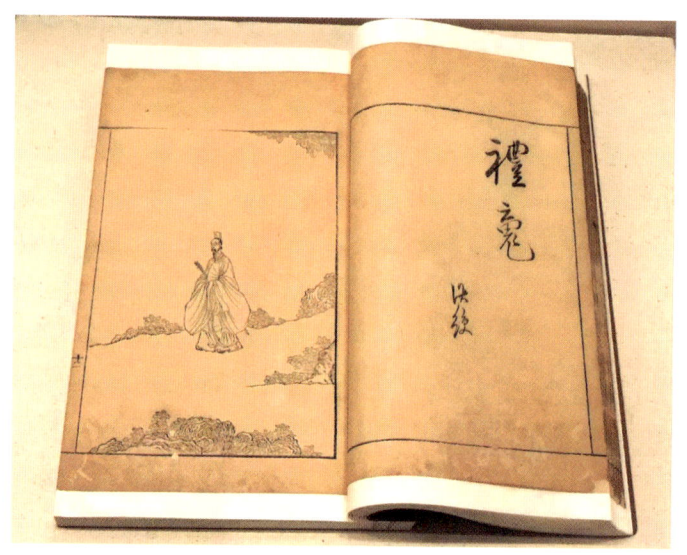

图 8-1　国家典籍博物馆：《楚辞五卷图一卷》（屈原等撰，来钦之述注）

　　明初的中央行政体制仍沿袭元朝旧制：设中书省统领六部、管理全国行政事务，另设有大都督府管理军事，御史台职掌监察，统称"三大府"。随着皇权与相权的冲突加剧，为了维护自己的统治，明太祖朱元璋借口谋反，于洪武十三年（1380 年）诛杀左丞相胡惟庸，废除中书省，自秦汉以来存在一千多年的丞相制度从此成为历史。此后朱元璋分相权于吏、户、礼、兵、刑、工六部，六部长官直接对皇帝负责。明代地方行政建制为省、府（州）、县三级。朱元璋废除了元朝的行省制度，改设布政司、都指挥使司和提刑按察使司，分别管理地方一级行政区的政务、军事和司法。在军事上，朱元璋还创立了卫所制，在全国重要的军事地区设卫，次要地方设所。

厂卫干预司法活动，是明朝司法制度的一个重要特点。厂，指东、西厂。东厂是明成祖所设；宪宗时，又设立西厂。卫，是指锦衣卫，依《明史·职官志》记载，锦衣卫掌侍卫、缉捕、刑狱等事，洪武十五年（1382年）设立。明太祖时曾动用"锦衣卫狱"审理大案，受株连者达数万人之多。明孝宗时，厂卫活动一度消沉。至武宗正德年间，复设西厂，当时东厂、西厂及锦衣卫首领多为太监刘瑾党羽，厂卫开始合流。在明代，东、西厂和锦衣卫往往相互勾结，残害忠良。名臣杨涟、左光斗皆因得罪权阉，惨死于锦衣卫狱。《明史·刑法志》称：*"刑法有创之自明，不衷古制者，廷杖、东西厂、锦衣卫、镇抚司狱是已。是数者，杀人至惨，而不丽于法。"*[1]

During the Ming Dynasty, administrative, legislative, judicial, and military powers were highly concentrated in the hands of the emperor, strengthening monarchical absolutism in ancient China. This centralization led to political corruption in the Ming Dynasty, which became especially rampant in its later years.

The central administrative system at the beginning of the Ming Dynasty still followed the model of the Yuan Dynasty—established the Central Secretariat to oversee the Six Ministries and manage national administrative affairs. Additionally, the Grand Military Commission was set up to manage military affairs, while the Censorate was responsible for supervision; these three institutions were collectively known as the "Three Great Offices." As the conflict between imperial power and the power of the chancellor intensified, Emperor Hongwu (Zhu Yuanzhang), in order to consolidate his rule, used the pretext of rebellion to execute the Left Chancellor Hu Weiyong in the thirteenth year of the Hongwu reign (1380) and abolished the Central Secretariat, ending the chancellery system that had existed for over a thousand years since the Qin and Han Dynasties. Zhu Yuanzhang divided the powers of the chancel-

---

〔1〕　参见朱勇主编：《中国法律史》，中国政法大学出版社2021年版，第246~265页。

lery among the Six Ministries (Personnel, Revenue, Rites, War, Punishments, and Works), whose ministers reported directly to the emperor. The local administrative system of the Ming Dynasty consisted of three levels: provinces, prefectures (or sub-prefectures), and counties. Zhu Yuanzhang abolished the Yuan Dynasty's provincial system and instead established provincial administrations: the Provincial Administration Commission, the Provincial Military Commission, and the Provincial Surveillance Commission, which respectively managed civil administration, military, and judicial matters. In military affairs, Zhu Yuanzhang also established the Wei-Suo system, setting up military units (Wei) in important regions and secondary units (Suo) in less critical areas.

Intervention by the Imperial Factories and Guards in judicial activities was a notable feature of the Ming judicial system. The "factories" refer to the Eastern Depot and the Western Depot. The Eastern Depot was established by Emperor Chengzu of the Ming Dynasty. During the reign of Emperor Xianzong, the Western Depot was set up. The "guards" refer to the Jinyiwei (Embroidered Uniform Guard). According to *The History of the Ming Dynasty: Records of Officials*, the Jinyiwei was established in the fifteenth year of the Hongwu reign (1382) to handle imperial guard duties, arrests, and prison investigations. Emperor Hongwu often used "The Jinyiwei Prison" to handle major cases, and the number of people implicated reached as many as tens of thousands. During Emperor Xiaozong's reign, the activities of the Imperial Factories and Guards once subsided, but in the Zhengde reign under Emperor Wuzong, the Western Depot was reinstated. At that time, most of the heads of the Eastern Depot, Western Depot, and the Jinyiwei were all partisans of the eunuch Liu Jin, and the Imperial Factories and Guards began to merge. During the Ming period, the Eastern Depot, the Western Depot and the Jinyiwei often colluded with each other, persecuting loyal officials and upright. Notable ministers such as Yang Lian and Zuo Guangdou both died tragically in The Jinyiwei Prison due to offending powerful eunuchs. According to *The History of the Ming Dynasty: Records of Penal Law*, "In the aspect of criminal law, practices that began in the Ming, diverging from ancient ones, include the court beatings, the Eastern Depot and the Western Depot, Jinyiwei, and Zhenfu prison; these methods killed people most cruelly, without conforming to legal norms and procedures."

 生词表

序号	生词	词性	汉语拼音	英文解释
1	沿袭	*v.*	yán xí	inherit
2	统领	*v.*	tǒng lǐng	command
3	职掌	*v.*	zhí zhǎng	charge
4	相权	*n.*	xiàng quán	the power of the prime minister
5	提刑按察使	*n.*	tí xíng àn chá shǐ	a judge of the Provincial Surveillance Commission
6	布政司	*n.*	bù zhèng sī	the bureau of provincial administration in the Ming Dynasty
7	卫所	*n.*	wèi suǒ	military garrison and station
8	厂卫	*n.*	chǎng wèi	eunuch spies and royal guards, the imperial espionage agencies of the Ming Dynasty
9	缉捕	*v.*	jī bǔ	arrest
10	党羽	*n.*	dǎng yǔ	henchmen
11	合流	*v.*	hé liú	merge，integrate

 导　读

　　明代的中央行政管理机构主要有内阁和"六部"，中央司法机关为刑部、都察院、大理寺。明朝司法制度的特色体现在基层"里老人理讼制度"和各

种名目的会审制度，而专制集权的发展对于司法制度也产生了深刻的影响，突出表现为东厂、西厂宦官和锦衣卫组织对于审判事务的参与和干涉。

课 文

《大明会典》是明朝一部具有行政法典性质的重要法律。明孝宗弘治十五年（1502 年）《大明会典》初步编成，但并未颁行。明武宗正德年间，《大明会典》经内阁重新审校、弥补疏漏后正式颁行天下，世称《正德会典》。此后会典又经世宗续纂（世称《嘉靖续纂会典》），及神宗重修（世称《万历重修会典》）。

中国政法大学法律古籍整理研究所

图 8-2　明·大明诏旨碑[1]

从内容上看，会典取材于明朝官修律、令、礼、式、宪纲和诸司档案书籍，内容广博，是集历朝法令、定一代章程的行政法典。《大明会典》的体例，基本沿袭《唐六典》，是以六部官制为纲，按宗人府、六部、都察院、六科、

---

〔1〕 转引自《法制文物日历｜二月九日·明·大明诏旨碑（曲阜孔庙）》，载"中国政法大学法律古籍整理研究所"公众号 2021 年 2 月 9 日，https://mp.weixin.qq.com/s/XM8ye5fOtuWyGCbVA5XEYQ，最后访问日期：2025 年 5 月 30 日。

各寺、府、监、司的次序，分述各行政机关的职掌和事例。与《唐六典》不同的是，《大明会典》是经钦命颁行、天下臣民共同遵守的法典，并非单纯的行政法规的汇编。它为清代"五朝会典"的制定奠定了基础，体现了明朝立法的重要成就。

明代的中央司法机关为刑部、都察院、大理寺，**"刑部受天下刑名，都察院纠察，大理寺驳正"**。刑部，专司审判之职，受理地方上诉案件、审核地方徒刑以上重案，审理京师地区和中央百官的案件。都察院，掌纠察，亦有司法权，在地方派驻监察御史巡视州县，审录罪囚。大理寺，掌复核，凡刑部所审案件，都须将案卷连同罪犯移送大理寺复核。重大疑难案件、死刑案件，由刑部、都察院和大理寺共同审理，由刑部先对案件提出初步判决意见，然后将案件移送大理寺复核，大理寺若认为判决不当，驳回重审。都察院则对整个审判过程进行监督，确保司法公正。若案件多次驳回仍未解决，则请求进行"九卿会审"，又称为"圆审"，由六部、通政使司、都察院和大理寺的最高领导会审；若案件仍无法解决，则奏请皇帝下旨处理，称为"制决"。

地方司法机关中，省一级由提刑按察使掌管一省刑名，有权处决刑罚为笞、杖的案件，徒刑以上重案则须报送刑部审核批准。府（州）、县二级由长官知府、知县兼掌审判事务。此外，明朝初期于基层乡里设立"申明亭"，由本乡人推举公直老人三五名，报官备案。里长、老人在申明亭受理民事案件和轻微刑事案件，如未经里长、老人处分而直接赴县起诉，视为越诉。

明朝的监察制度十分完善。1382年，明太祖把御史台更名为都察院，号为"天子耳目风纪之司"，负责弹劾大臣结党乱政、百官败坏风纪，朝觐、考核时会同吏部考察官员升降，遇重大案件会同刑部、大理寺审理案件。都察院长官为左、右都御史，下设左、右副都御史，以及左、右金都御史。明朝又在地方设立十三道监察御史，负责纠正和弹劾中央及地方所有官员的违法行为。为了保证监察权得以实施，发挥它的应有作用，明代还非常注重监察立法工作，如洪武年间的《宪纲总例》《巡抚六察》《巡按六察》，明英宗时期的《宪纲条例》，以及《大明会典》中有关监察的部分等。这些法规规范了监察活动，使监察制度更加完备和系统。[1]

 生词表

序号	生词	词性	汉语拼音	英文解释
1	内阁	n.	nèi gé	imperial cabinet
2	都察院	n.	dū chá yuàn	the censorate in the Ming Dynasty
3	大理寺	n.	dà lǐ sì	the supreme court of the Ming Dynasty
4	弥补	v.	mí bǔ	compensate, remedy
5	疏漏	n.	shū lòu	careless omission
6	续纂	v.	xù zuǎn	continue to compilation
7	宪纲	n.	xiàn gāng	legal framework
8	档案	n.	dàng àn	archives
9	奠定	v.	diàn dìng	establish
10	刑名	n.	xíng míng	criminal cases and legal matters
11	纠察	v.	jiū chá	supervise and rectify
12	驳正	v.	bó zhèng	refute and correct
13	圆审	n.	yuán shěn	the judicial review system in the Ming Dynasty
14	制决	n.	zhì jué	the emperor's ruling by decree
15	里长	n.	lǐ zhǎng	head of a group of households
16	越诉	n.	yuè sù	the act of appealing beyond the level of authority
17	耳目	n.	ěr mù	one who spies for somebody else
18	风纪	n.	fēng jì	conduct and discipline
19	弹劾	v.	tán hé	impeach
20	朝觐	v.	cháo jìn	have an audience with an emperor

---

[1] 参见朱勇主编：《中国法律史》，中国政法大学出版社 2021 年版，第 246~265 页。

重点汉字【讯】

　　讯，汉语一级字。此字始见于商代甲骨文，其古字形像一人反缚其手，临之以口，表审讯之义。"讯"本义指问，特指审问、审讯。由询问之义引申指询问的内容，即音讯、音信，因此"讯"又可指书信。

图 8-3　"讯"字篆刻（王琦 刻）

 汉字拓展

序号	词汇	汉语拼音	英文解释	例句
1	审讯	shěn xùn	trial	此案尚在审讯中，未能结案。
2	传讯	chuán xùn	summon for interrogation or trial	先后传讯过三次，都是报馆主笔出庭的。
3	问讯	wèn xùn	greet	逢年过节，大家总要彼此问讯。
4	讯实	xùn shí	be proved true by trial	犯人终于供认讯实，案件得以真相大白。
5	讯号	xùn hào	signal	部队正在等待总进攻的讯号。
6	音讯	yīn xùn	tidings	我许多年没得到她的音讯了。
7	讯息	xùn xī	message	他离开家有两年时间没有讯息了。
8	通讯	tōng xùn	communicate	遇难航班早已失去全部通讯能力。

化知识【郑和下西洋】

　　明代永乐、宣德年间，三宝太监郑和受皇帝委派率领船队先后七次远赴西太平洋和印度洋航行。首次航行始于永乐三年（1405 年），末次航行结束于宣德八年（1433 年），历时 28 年。由于使团正使由郑和担任，且船队航行至婆罗洲以西洋面（即明代所谓"西洋"），故该历史事件史称"郑和下西洋"。

　　在七次航行中，郑和船队多在江苏省太仓市的刘家港集结正式出发，至福建省福州市长乐太平港驻泊伺风开洋，一共拜访了 30 多个国家和地区，其中包括爪哇、苏门答腊、苏禄、彭亨、真腊、古里、暹罗、榜葛剌、阿丹、天方、左法尔、忽鲁谟斯、木骨都束等地，已知最远到达东非、红海。

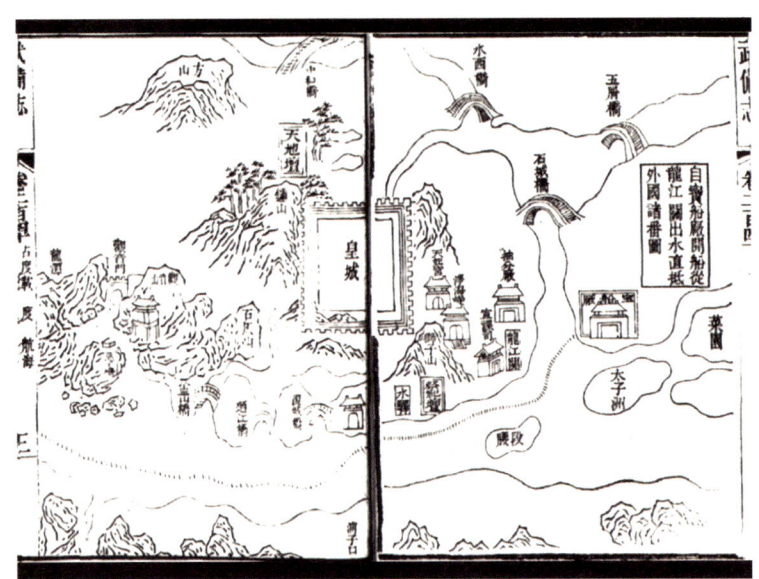

图 8-4　《〈郑和航海图〉之南京图》[1]

　　郑和下西洋是中国古代规模最大、船只和海员最多、时间最久的海上航行，也是在欧洲"地理大发现"以前世界历史上规模最大的海上探险活动。

――――――――――――

　　〔1〕转引自林梅村：《观沧海：大航海时代诸文明的冲突与交流》，上海古籍出版社 2018 年版，第 64 页。

郑和下西洋，在古代中国对外关系史和航海史上都是罕见的壮举，它增进了中国同亚非各国的友好交往和经济文化的交流。

法 治文物【《加封圣母制书碑》】

《加封圣母制书碑》是明代重要的历史文物。现存于山西省太原市晋祠，碑阳额题"福由心造"，阴额题"广增福田"，额、身石质不一，应该不是原配。碑阳刻洪武二年（1369 年）十二月制书，10 行，满行 25 字。第 10 行"年"字左侧有"宝"字以替代原制书上的玺印。内容载当年"春夏之间，天久不雨，遣使遍祭于山川原隰之神"，因在太原向显灵昭济圣母祈雨"有应"，皇帝特加封其为"广惠显灵昭济圣母"。碑阴为立碑官员题名。

图 8-5 《加封圣母制书碑》[1]

〔1〕 参见《明·〈加封圣母制书〉》，载中国政法大学中华法制文明虚拟博物馆，https://flgj.cupl.edu.cn/info/1072/4350.htm，最后访问日期：2024 年 11 月 22 日。

碑文中的"圣母"指邑姜，即姜子牙之女、周武王之妻，周成王及唐叔虞的母亲。宋熙宁十年（1077年）封"昭济圣母"，政和元年（1111年）加封"显灵昭济圣母"。明洪武二年加封"广惠显灵昭济圣母"，洪武四年（1371年）改号为"晋源之神"。清同治八年（1869年）加封号"广惠显灵昭济沛泽圣母"，光绪五年（1879年）加封号"广惠显灵昭济沛泽翊化圣母"。

经 典阅读

《明大诰》序

朕闻曩古历代君臣，当天下之大任，闵生民之涂炭。立纲陈纪，昭示天下，为民造福。当是时，君臣同心，志同一气，所以感皇天后土之监，海岳效灵，由是雨旸时若，五谷丰登，家给人足。斯君臣之逝，遐且久矣。育民之功，载诸方册，犹如见存。君子读诵至斯，陡然情怀感激，仰慕于千万古之下，恨不目击耳闻，乐此升平，以为庆幸。

昔者元处华夏，实非华夏之仪，所以九十三年之治，华风沦没，彝道倾颓。学者以经书专记熟为奇。其持心操节，必格神人之道，略不究衷。所以临事之际，私胜公微，以致愆深旷海，罪重巍山。当犯之期，弃市之尸未移，新犯大辟者即至。若此乖为覆身灭姓，见存者曾几人而格非。

呜呼！果朕不才而致是欤？抑前代污染而有此欤？然况由人心不古，致使而然。今将害民事理，昭示天下。诸司敢有不务公而务私，在外贼贪酷虐吾民者，穷其原而搜罪之。斯令一出，世世守行之。洪武十八年十月朔序。

 参考译文

我听说古时历代的君主和臣子，承担治理天下的重任，关心人民的疾苦。他们建立规范和秩序，向全天下明示，为人民创造福利。在那时，君主和臣子心意相合，意志一致。因此感动了天地的神灵，海山显灵，因而雨水适时，五谷丰收，家家户户都有足够的食物。这样的君臣，他们虽已离去很久，但养育百姓的功绩被记录在历史册页上，好像还在眼前一样。读到这里，突然感到激动和感激，仰慕那些千古以来的典范，遗憾自己未能亲眼见到、亲耳听到，能在那样的盛世生活，真是太幸运了。

过去元代统治华夏，但其行为并不符合华夏的礼仪，因此九十三年的统治导致华夏的文化风尚衰败，礼仪道德崩溃。学者们把精力放在死记硬背经书上，认为这是才能的体现。但对于思想品德必然违背天理人情，却不深究其中的真意。因此，在处理事务时，私欲膨胀、公心衰退，以致过错比大海深，罪恶比高山重。犯罪的时候，被处死的尸体还未搬走，新犯死罪的人就已被送到刑场。如此违背正道导致自己丧生、全家覆灭，可是，现在有几个人能因此改正错误？

呜呼！是我的无能导致了这种局面吗？还是由于前代的不良风气导致的呢？可能还是因为人心不如古时导致的。现在将危害民众的事实向全天下公示：所有官员如果不是为公而为私，在外贪污受贿，残忍对待我的人民，都应该追根溯源，彻查其罪行。这样的命令一旦发布，世世代代都应遵守执行。洪武十八年十月初一作序。

I have heard that in ancient times, emperors and their ministers undertook the great responsibility of governing the world and were concerned about the suffering of their people. They established norms and records to clearly demonstrate to the world their intentions to benefit the populace. At such times, the emperors and their ministers were united in heart and spirit. Thus, they moved the spirits of heaven and earth, causing seas and mountains to manifest their power, leading to timely rains and abundant harvests, ensuring that every household was well provided for. Those emperors and ministers, though long gone, left legacies of nurturing the people that are recorded in historical documents, almost as if they were still present. When gentlemen read these accounts, they are suddenly moved and grateful, admiring these exemplars from millennia past, regretting that they could not witness such times of peace and prosperity themselves. It's lucky to live in such a prosperous world.

In the past, the Yuan Dynasty ruled over China but did not adhere to Chinese rituals, resulting in ninety-three years of governance during which Chinese cultural norms and moral disciplines declined. Scholars focused solely on rote memorization of the classics, considering it a talent. However, they didn't delve into the true meaning of the fact that their moral character and thoughts are bound to go against the principles of sages. Hence, when it came to handling practical affairs, personal interests expanded while public duty declined, leading to profound mistakes and heavy sins. When crimes were committed, the bodies in the execution ground were not yet cleared before new death row prisoners arrived. Acting so against the right path had led to their own deaths and the downfall of their entire families. However, nowadays, how many people can actually correct their own faults because of this?

Alas! Is it my incompetence that has led to this state? Or is it the corrupt influences of previous generations that have caused this situation? Perhaps it is due to modern people lack the simplicity and integrity of the ancients. Now the facts that will endanger people are publicized to the public: If any official dares to prioritize personal gain over public duty, indulge in corruption and be cruel to my people, they should be thoroughly investigated and their crimes unearthed. Once this decree is issued, it should be upheld for generations. Proclaimed on the first day of the tenth lunar month, in the eighteenth year of Hongwu.

课 后练习

1. 选择题：明太祖朱元璋于洪武十三年诛杀左丞相胡惟庸，废除_____，自秦汉以来存在一千多年的丞相制度从此成为历史。

A. 御史大夫

B. 内阁

C. 中书省

D. 太尉

2. 判断题：《大明会典》是明朝重要的行政法典，也是一部单纯的行政法规汇编。

3. 填空题：朱元璋废除了元朝的行省制度，改设布政司、_____和_____，分别管理政务、军事和司法。

4. 简答题：请简述《大明会典》的体例。

5. 讨论题：明朝的行政、立法、司法和军事等权力均集中于皇帝一人之手，请思考明朝的统治者都采取了哪些制度以实现权力的高度集中？其中哪些制度是明朝独有的？又产生了哪些严重后果？

课 文参考翻译

The "Code of Great Ming Dynasty" was an important administrative code of the Ming Dynasty. Initially compiled in the 15th year of the Hongzhi reign of Emperor Xiaozong (1502), it was not promulgated until the reign of Emperor Wuzong, during the Zhengde period, after being reexamined and revised by the Imperial Cabinet to fill the omissions. This revised version was known as "Code of Zhengde Period" in history. Later, further revisions were made during the reign of Emperor Shizong (known as "Continued Compilation of Jiajing Period" in history), and again under Emperor Shenzong (known as "Revised Compilation of Wanli Period" in history).

In terms of its content, the Code drew from the Ming Dynasty's official statutes, decrees, rituals, procedures, constitutional codes and archives from various departments, offering a comprehensive administrative code that consolidated laws and regulations from previous dynasties. The format of the "Code of Great Ming Dynasty" primarily followed that of the "Six Institutions of Tang Dynasty," organized according to the six ministries system, detailing the responsibilities and cases handled by each administrative body, from the Imperial Clansmen's Office, the Six Ministries, the Censorate, the Six Offices of Scrutiny, various temples, prefectures, directorates and departments. Unlike the "Six Institutions of Tang Dynasty," the

"Code of Great Ming Dynasty" was an officially mandated code that all subjects of the empire were required to follow, not merely a compilation of administrative regulations. It laid the groundwork for "Comprehensive Statutes of Five Dynasties" in the Qing Dynasty and marked a significant legislative achievement of the Ming Dynasty.

The central judicial organs in the Ming Dynasty included the Ministry of Punishments, the Censorate, and the Court of Judicial Review. "The Ministry of Punishments handles all criminal cases across the country, the Censorate is responsible for oversight, and the Court of Judicial Review reviews and corrects judicial decisions." The Ministry of Punishments was responsible for trials, accepting local appeals, reviewing serious local cases (penal servitude or above), and trying cases in the capital and those involving central officials. The Censorate, with investigatory and judicial powers, sent censors to local areas to inspect prisons. The Court of Judicial Review was responsible for re-examining cases handled by the Ministry of Punishments. For this purpose, the Ministry was required to transfer both case files and the accused to the Court for review. For major or capital cases, the three organs conducted joint trials. The Ministry of Punishments proposed a preliminary verdict, then transferred the case to the Court of Judicial Review. If the revision was deemed improper, the case was sent back for retrial. The Censorate supervised the process. If the case remained unresolved after multiple retrials, a "Joint Trial by Nine Ministers" (or "Round Trial") was held by the heads of the Six Ministries, the General Office of Communications, the Censorate, and the Court of Judicial Review. If still unresolved, it was submitted to the emperor for an "Imperial Decision" .

At the provincial level, the Provincial Surveillance Commissioner handled local criminal cases, sentencing flogging and beating cases and reporting serious ones to the Ministry of Punishments. Prefects and magistrates at the prefecture and county levels handled trials. In the early Ming Dynasty, "Exemplary Pavilions" were set up in rural areas. Elders recommended by locals accepted civil and minor criminal cases. Bypassing them for direct county-level lawsuits was considered improper.

The Ming Dynasty also advanced its surveillance system. In 1382, the founding emperor renamed the Imperial Censorate（御史台）to the Censorate（都察院）, which was known as the "department for the emperor's eyes and ears and the maintenance of discipline." It was tasked with impeaching ministers for factionalism and corruption. During court audiences and performance appraisals, this office worked with the Ministry of Personnel to assess and promote or demotion of officials, and in major cases, it collaborated with the Ministry of Punishments and the Court of Judicial Review. The Censorate was headed by the left and right censors, under whom were left and right deputy and left and right associate censors. The Ming Dynasty also established thirteen circuits for censors to correct and impeach unlawful acts of officials inside and outside the court. To ensure the efficacy of the surveillance system and its legislative backbone, the Ming Dynasty placed great emphasis on legislating for oversight. For example, during the Hongwu reign, there were "General Provisions of the Constitutional Statutes," "Six Inspections by Provincial Inspectors," "Six Inspections by Circuit Inspectors," the "Regulations of the Constitutional Statutes" during the reign of Emperor Yingzong, and the relevant supervisory parts in "Code of Great Ming Dynasty." These measures made the surveillance system more comprehensive and systematic.

明朝时期的法律（三）

课 前准备

明朝从英宗以后进入由盛转衰的中后期，政治制度和立法思想已经没有明朝初建时期洋溢的进取精神，而是趋向于保守，君主专制空前加强。到了明朝晚期，政治腐败、宦官专权、朝臣党争、土地高度兼并，农民起义不断，明朝统治逐步走向衰落。

"洪武通宝"金币
"Hongwu Tongbao" gold coin
明·洪武

图 9-1　山东博物馆：明·"洪武通宝"金币

面对纲纪败坏、盗贼四起的现实，一批正直的官员兼思想家主张明礼义、正纲纪、礼法结合，力图挽狂澜于既倒。如明代中期思想家丘浚认为：**"人道之所以立者，以其有此礼也"**。明代著名思想家王守仁（世人也多称其为王阳明）是"心学"的集大成者，他把"良知"、"天理"和"礼"统一于一体，提倡通过"致良知"来实现封建礼治。为了恢复和振兴封建礼治，他们都提倡以礼义教化百姓。丘浚指出：**"为治之道二，政与教而已，政有纲纪，教有枢要。"**王守仁特别推崇孟子所主张的**"善政不如善教之得民也"**，因而提倡**"以教化当干戈"**。上述明礼义、正纲纪的思想，对于明朝的法制建设有着一定的影响，《问刑条例》中便有相应的规定。然而社会矛盾的严峻，也使得思想家们在倡导以礼义教化人心的同时，深知只凭一般的礼义说教不会得到理想的效果，必须礼法结合，互相为用。[1]

The Ming Dynasty entered a period of decline from the reign of Emperor Yingzong onwards. The political system and legislative thoughts lacked the progressive spirit of the dynasty's founding era and turned towards conservatism, with unprecedented strengthening of absolute monarchy. By the late Ming period, political corruption, eunuch dominance, factional conflicts among court officials, and high concentration of land ownership led to continual peasant uprisings and a gradual decline of the Ming Dynasty's rule.

Faced with the deterioration of public order and rampant theft, a group of upright official-thinkers emphasized the importance of proper rites and rituals, correct standards, and the combination of ritual and law in an effort to reverse the dire situation. For instance, the mid-Ming thinker Qiu Jun stated, "In the establishment of human relations, nothing precedes rites." Wang Shouren, also known as Wang Yangming, was a renowned thinker of the Ming Dynasty and the master who synthesized and brought the "School of the Mind" to its culmination. He integrated "conscience," "natural law," and "rites" into a unified concept. He advocated for the realization of feudal ritual governance through "extending innate knowledge." To restore and revitalize feudal ritual governance, they all advocated for the moral education of the populace with rites and righteousness. Qiu Jun noted, "The way of governance lies not beyond administration and education, with administration having its principles and education its pivotal essentials." Wang Shouren particularly revered Mencius's view that "good governance is less effective in winning people's hearts than good education," thus he promoted "education over warfare." The ideas of upholding rites and righ-

---

〔1〕　参见张晋藩主编：《中国法律史》，中国政法大学出版社 2019 年版，第 351 页。

teousness, and correcting standards had a certain impact on the legal construction of the Ming Dynasty, as reflected in the "Regulations on Criminal Trials." However, the severity of social contradictions also made the thinkers realize that mere preaching of rites and righteousness would not be effective without integrating these principles with laws, using them mutually.

 生词表

序号	生词	词性	汉语拼音	英文解释
1	由盛转衰	*phr.*	yóu shèng zhuǎn shuāi	from prosperity to decline
2	洋溢	*v.*	yáng yì	brim, overflow
3	进取	*adj.*	jìn qǔ	enterprising
4	朝臣	*n.*	cháo chén	court councillor
5	党争	*n.*	dǎng zhēng	factional strife
6	纲纪	*n.*	gāng jì	principles and discipline
7	盗贼四起	*idm.*	dào zéi sì qǐ	rampant thievery
8	正直	*adj.*	zhèng zhí	upright, honest
9	礼义	*n.*	lǐ yì	propriety and righteousness
10	礼法结合	*phr.*	lǐ fǎ jié hé	integration of rites and laws
11	挽狂澜于既倒	*idm.*	wǎn kuáng lán yú jì dǎo	save a dire situation
12	致良知	*phr.*	zhì liáng zhī	realize one's innate conscience
13	礼治	*n.*	lǐ zhì	rule by ritual
14	教有枢要	*phr.*	jiào yǒu shū yào	education focusing on key essentials
15	善政	*n.*	shàn zhèng	good governance
16	法制建设	*phr.*	fǎ zhì jiàn shè	legal system construction
17	社会矛盾	*phr.*	shè huì máo dùn	social contradiction
18	互相为用	*phr.*	hù xiāng wéi yòng	be mutually beneficial

导 读

　　《大明律》在内容上大体沿袭唐律。相比较而言，事关典礼及风俗教化的罪行，唐律规定的处罚重于明律；而有关贼盗及帑项钱粮的犯罪，明律规定的处罚重于唐律。清代薛允升把这种差异归结为："古人先礼教而后刑法，后世则重刑法而轻礼教。"

课 文

　　明朝中叶以后，《大明律》颁行已历百年，社会政治、经济情况与明初相比已发生很大变化，定律虽不能轻易修改，但社会变化必须通过法律调整予以适应，《问刑条例》的制定满足了这一需要。明代历朝通过修订《问刑条例》，对《大明律》作出适当的补充和修正。这样既保持了正律的稳定性，又及时反映社会生活的变化，有利于法律的实施。但在司法实践中，皇权专制条件下以例破律的情况并不少见，这同样也是不容忽视的。

　　《大明律》是在明太祖不断加强专制集权的背景下编撰的，体现了朱元璋重典治世和严于治吏的精神，主要表现为四方面：①加重对谋反、谋大逆等重罪的处罚。"谋反""谋大逆"是封建社会最为严重的犯罪，直接危害皇帝的统治，历代政权均予以重惩。依照《大明律》的规定，凡谋反及谋大逆，只要是同谋，不分首犯从犯一律凌迟处死，犯人的祖父、父亲、子孙、兄弟以及伯叔父、兄弟之子，甚至异姓同居之人，不论是否同籍，只要年纪在十六岁以上，不论是否残疾，一律处斩；上述亲属中，十五岁以下男子以及母女、妻妾、姐妹，包括儿媳等，均罚没给功臣当奴婢，财产没入官府。知情故纵以及窝藏包庇者也要处斩。②严禁臣下结党。鉴于历代权臣结党造成皇权削弱、最终导致政治危机的教训，明朝严禁臣下结党，在《大明律》中增设了前代刑法中所没有的"奸党"罪，并罗列了"奸党"罪的种种表现。③严惩官吏职务犯罪。明太祖十分注意整顿吏治，这种思想也影响了明代立法。《明大诰》已经向后人展示了当时惩贪法律的严酷性。在定型的《大明律》

中，惩治官吏的贪污受贿仍是十分重要的内容。④加大打击强盗、窃盗行为的力度。明律规定，只要实行强盗行为，即便不得财，也要杖一百、流三千里，但凡得财，不论首犯从犯，一律处斩。万历年间的《问刑条例》规定："**强盗杀人，放火烧人房屋，奸污人妻女，打劫牢狱、仓库及干系城池衙门，并积至百人以上，不分曾否得财，俱照得财律，处斩。**"关于窃盗之罪，唐代盗窃罪没有死刑，明代则不同，规定犯盗窃罪三次者就要被处以绞刑。

图 9-2　山东博物馆：明·九缝皮弁

　　明代刑罚的种类沿用了唐律的五刑制度，以笞、杖、徒、流、死为法定刑。"廷杖"是明朝皇帝处罚大臣的一种特殊刑罚，明太祖朱元璋开启先河，武宗后习以为常。据《明史·刑法志》记载，明武宗"南巡之争"中，皇帝一次廷杖一百四十六人，杖死十一人。明世宗"大礼议之争"中，皇帝廷杖一百三十四人，杖死十六人。[1]

―――――――――

〔1〕 参见朱勇主编：《中国法律史》，中国政法大学出版社 2021 年版，第 251~258 页。

生词表

序号	生词	词性	汉语拼音	英文解释
1	颁行	*v.*	bān xíng	promulgate
2	结党	*v.*	jié dǎng	form factions
3	奸党	*n.*	jiān dǎng	treacherous cliques
4	职务犯罪	*phr.*	zhí wù fàn zuì	official misconduct
5	惩贪	*phr.*	chéng tān	punish corruption
6	受贿	*v.*	shòu huì	accept bribes
7	强盗	*n.*	qiáng dào	robber
8	窃盗	*n.*	qiè dào	theft
9	绞刑	*n.*	jiǎo xíng	hanging（execution）
10	法定刑	*n.*	fǎ dìng xíng	statutory punishment
11	廷杖	*n.*	tíng zhàng	imperial beating
12	先河	*n.*	xiān hé	precedent

重点汉字【盗】

图 9-3　"盗"字篆刻（王琦 刻）

　　盗，汉语一级字。此字始见于商代甲骨文。盗的本义是偷、偷窃，引申指偷东西的人，又指强盗。此外，"盗"除了指偷窃财物，也可指窃取名声。

汉字拓展

序号	词汇	汉语拼音	英文解释	例句
1	盗窃	dào qiè	theft，steal	警方逮捕了几名涉嫌盗窃的嫌疑人。
2	盗贼	dào zéi	thief，robber	那个盗贼被抓后交还了所有赃物。
3	偷盗	tōu dào	steal	他因多次偷盗而被判刑。
4	盗版	dào bǎn	pirated version	市场上充斥着盗版软件。
5	盗用	dào yòng	embezzle，misappropriate	他因盗用公款而被解雇。
6	盗窃罪	dào qiè zuì	crime of theft	他因犯盗窃罪被判入狱。
7	盗卖	dào mài	sell stolen goods	有人因涉嫌盗卖文物被捕。
8	盗掘	dào jué	unauthorized digging	该团伙专门盗掘古墓。
9	盗猎	dào liè	poach	他们被指控盗猎濒危野生动物。
10	防盗	fáng dào	anti-theft	他们为新车安装了最新的防盗系统。

文 化知识【吴承恩与《西游记》】

《西游记》是中国古代四大名著之一，由明代文学家吴承恩创作。《西游记》的故事取材自历史上唐代高僧玄奘西行印度求取佛经的真实事迹。

小说虽然以真实的佛教取经故事为蓝本，但在小说中，这一历史事件被融入了大量的神话、佛教、道教以及民间传说，塑造了以玄奘为原型的唐僧，以及他的三个徒弟——孙悟空、猪八戒、沙僧，师徒四人一起经历了艰难险阻，最终完成了取经任务的奇幻故事。

《西游记》全书共 100 回，前 7 回主要叙述孙悟空的出身和他大闹天宫等的叛逆行为。第 8 回至第 12 回介绍了唐僧的来历。第 13 回到第 99 回则以"九九八十一难"为主要线索，讲述师徒四人经历的各种磨难，包括与妖魔鬼怪的斗争，故事情节跌宕起伏。第100回师徒四人终成正果，取得真经。

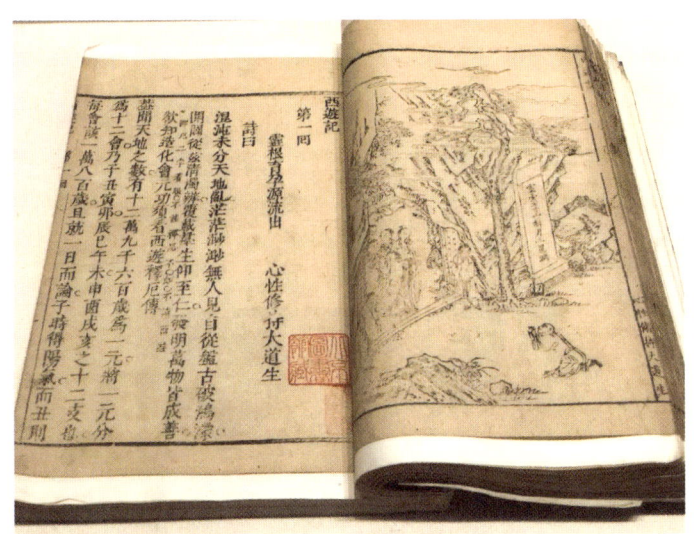

图 9-4 国家典籍博物馆:《西游记》明刻本

《西游记》表面上是一部冒险小说，但其深层次的主题涉及多方面的哲学和宗教思想，主要围绕佛教、道教的教义展开。书中展现了人类对理想世界的追求，反映了人性中的善与恶、意志与欲望的冲突。它对中国的文化、宗教和文学都产生了深远的影响。其生动的情节和人物形象不仅在文学上成为经典，还通过戏剧、影视、动画等多种形式传承下来。尤其是孙悟空这个角色，他勇敢、机智、叛逆的形象深受大众喜爱，成为中国民间文化中无数故事的原型。

此外，《西游记》还影响了许多外国文学和影视作品。作为奇幻文学的典范，它启发了世界各国的作家和艺术家，推动了跨文化交流。

法 治文物【《孟氏宗传祖图碑》】

此碑为明代所立，碑高214厘米，宽86厘米，厚24厘米，基座高40厘米。碑额为梯形。碑身两面各以书页的形式刻12组内容，每组分左右两图，配有顺序号及说明，以连环画圣迹图的形式再现了孟子一生的主要活动，实为《孟氏祖庭》一书的石刻本。其中一面自上而下刻《孟子圣迹图》12幅，内容依次为断机、梁惠王问利国、齐宣王问治国、传食于诸侯、门人、公孙丑问浩然、乐正克配享、道性善、邾国公及邾国宣献夫人、思孟传授、四基山坟庙图、亚圣公夫人。另一面上部刻邹县城郭图、宋南门外庙制图、大元重修庙制图、马鞍山林墓图、邹国图及配享宣圣位次文，下部刻《孟氏家传祖图始末之记》，金大安三年（1211年）所作的《孟氏家谱序》及该书的目录。

图 9-5 《孟氏宗传祖图碑》[1]

《孟子圣迹图》记录了孟子一生的主要事迹及历代对孟子的封谥、孟子的师承关系等，是研究孟子生平事迹及古代县制、庙制变迁的珍贵史料。

---

〔1〕 参见《明·〈孟氏宗传祖图碑〉》，载中国政法大学中华法制文明虚拟博物馆，https://flgj.cupl.edu.cn/info/1072/4348.htm，最后访问日期：2024年12月6日。

经 典阅读

《西游记》第一回：灵根育孕源流出 心性修持大道生（节选）

诗曰：混沌未分天地乱，茫茫渺渺无人见。自从盘古破鸿蒙，开辟从兹清浊辨。覆载群生仰至仁，发明万物皆成善。欲知造化会元功，须看《西游释厄传》。

盖闻天地之数，有十二万九千六百岁为一元。将一元分为十二会，乃子、丑、寅、卯、辰、巳、午、未、申、酉、戌、亥之十二支也。每会该一万八百岁。且就一日而论：子时得阳气，而丑则鸡鸣；寅不通光，而卯则日出；辰时食后，而巳则挨排；日午天中，而未则西蹉；申时晡而日落酉；戌黄昏而人定亥。譬于大数，若到戌会之终，则天地昏曚而万物否矣。再去五千四百岁，交亥会之初，则当黑暗，而两间人物俱无矣，故曰混沌。又五千四百岁，亥会将终，贞下起元，近子之会，而复逐渐开明。邵康节曰："冬至子之半，天心无改移。一阳初动处，万物未生时。"到此，天始有根。再五千四百岁，正当子会，轻清上腾，有日，有月，有星，有辰。日、月、星、辰，谓之四象。故曰，天开于子。又经五千四百岁，子会将终，近丑之会，而逐渐坚实。《易》曰："大哉乾元！至哉坤元！万物资生，乃顺承天。"至此，地始凝结。再五千四百岁，正当丑会，重浊下凝，有水，有火，有山，有石，有土。水、火、山、石、土，谓之五形。故曰，地辟于丑。又经五千四百岁，丑会终而寅会之初，发生万物。历曰："天气下降，地气上升；天地交合，群物皆生。"至此，天清地爽，阴阳交合。再五千四百岁，正当寅会，生人，生兽，生禽，正谓天地人，三才定位。故曰，人生于寅。

◆ 参考译文

The poem says: Chaos unseparated, heaven and earth were in turmoil, vast and indistinct, no one could see. Since Pangu broke open the primordial confusion, the world was divided, and clear from turbid was distinguished. All beings rely on the great benevolence of heaven and earth, all things manifest and naturally incline toward good. If you wish to know the secret of creation, you must read *The Journey to the West.*

It is said that the cycle of heaven and earth spans 129 600 years, which is called one "yuan." One yuan is divided into twelve "hui," corresponding to the twelve earthly branches: Zi, Chou, Yin, Mao, Chen, Si, Wu, Wei, Shen, You, Xu, and Hai. Each "hui" spans 10 800 years. Let's consider one day as an analogy: at Zi hour (11PM-1AM), the positive energy begins to rise; at Chou hour (1AM-3AM), the rooster crows; at Yin hour (3AM-5AM), light is not yet visible; at Mao hour (5AM-7AM), the sun rises; at Chen hour (7AM-9AM), people have breakfast; at Si hour (9AM-11AM), the day's work starts; at Wu hour (11AM-1PM), the sun is at its zenith; at Wei hour (1PM-3PM), the sun begins its westward decline; at Shen hour (3PM-5PM), it is late afternoon; at You hour (5PM-7PM), the sun sets; at Xu hour (7PM-9PM), twilight arrives; at Hai hour (9PM-11PM), people rest. If we compare this to the grand cycle, at the end of the Xu hui, heaven and earth are shrouded in darkness, and all beings perish. After another 5400 years, the beginning of the Hai hui marks the period of total darkness when neither heaven nor earth contains any living beings—this is called "chaos." Another 5400 years later, as the Hai hui ends, a new cycle begins during the Zi hui, and gradually, light starts to appear again. The philosopher Shao Kangjie once said, "In the middle of the winter solstice at Zi hour, heaven's heart does not shift. At the moment when positive energy first stirs, nothing has yet been born." At this point, the sky begins to have a foundation. After another 5400 years, at the height of the Zi hui, the light and clear energy rises, creating the sun, moon, stars, and constellations, collectively called the "four symbols." Therefore, it is said that heaven was opened in the Zi hui. Another 5400 years pass, and as the Zi hui ends and nears the Chou hui, the world gradually solidifies. The *I-Ching* says, "Great is the power of Qianyuan (Heaven); immense is the power of Kunyuan (Earth). All things are born and grow, following the will of Heaven and Earth." At this point, the earth begins to condense. Another 5400 years later, in the middle of the Chou hui, the heavy and dense energy sinks, forming water, fire, mountains, rocks, and soil, collectively known as the "five forms." Therefore, it is said that the earth was created during the Chou hui. After another 5400 years, as the Chou hui ends and the Yin hui begins, life starts to grow. The calendar states, "Heaven's energy descends, and earth's energy rises; heaven and earth interact, and all creatures are born." By this point, the heavens are clear, and the earth is bright, with the forces of yin and yang in balance. After another 5400 years, at the height of the Yin hui, humans, animals, and birds are born. This is the moment when heaven, earth, and humanity—the three talents—are fully established. Therefore, it is said that humanity was born in the Yin hui.

课 后练习

1. 选择题：《大明律》颁行百年之后，为了适应社会变化，历朝通过修定_____，对《大明律》作出适当的补充和修正。

A.《明会典》

B.《问刑条例》

C.《大诰》

D.《大明律例》

2. 判断题：明朝随着商品经济的发展，私有观念越来越强，开始出现专门的民事立法。

3. 填空题：《大明律》在内容上大体沿袭唐律，相比较而言，事关_____的罪行，唐律规定的处罚重于明律；而有关_____及帑项钱粮的犯罪，明律规定的处罚重于唐律。

4. 简答题：明朝中后期，面对纲纪败坏、盗贼四起的现实，一批正直的官员兼思想家强调明礼义、正纲纪、礼法结合，请简述一到两位思想家的代表性观点。

5. 讨论题：《大明律》是在明太祖不断加强专制集权的背景下编纂的，请论述其中哪些具体方面体现了朱元璋重典治世和严于治吏的精神？

（课）文参考翻译

    After the mid-Ming period, "Statutes of Great Ming Dynasty" had been in effect for over a hundred years. During this period, significant changes occurred in social politics and economic situations compared to the early Ming period. Although the Statutes should not be changed lightly, it was essential for social changes to be adapted through legal adjustments. The formulation of "Regulations on Criminal Trials" met this need. Throughout the dynasties, the Regulations were revised to properly supplement and amend "Statutes of Great Ming Dynasty." This approach not only maintained the stability of the official law but also timely reflected changes in social life, facilitating the implementation of the law. However, in judicial practice, it was common for precedents to override the law under the conditions of absolute monarchy, a situation that cannot be ignored.

    "Statutes of Great Ming Dynasty" was compiled under the background of Emperor Hongwu's continuous strengthening of autocratic centralization, reflecting his spirit of strict governance and harsh management of officials, manifested in four aspects:

    (1) Aggravate punishment for serious crimes such as rebellion and great treason. "rebellion" and "great treason" were considered the most severe crimes in feudal society, directly threatening the emperor's rule. All dynasties severely punished such offenses. According to "Statutes of Great Ming Dynasty," anyone involved in planning a rebellion or great treason, whether as a principal or an accomplice, was to be brutally executed by dismemberment. The convict's grandfather, father, sons, grandsons, and uncles and their sons, even non-relatives living together,

regardless of whether they shared the same household registration, if aged sixteen or older and irrespective of any disabilities, were to be executed; others under fifteen, as well as mothers, daughters, wives, concubines, and sisters, including daughters-in-law, were sentenced to servitude, with all property confiscated by the state. Those who knowingly harbored or concealed such criminals were also executed.

(2) Strictly forbid ministers to form factions. Given the historical lessons of powerful ministers forming factions that weakened imperial power and led to political crises, the Ming Dynasty strictly prohibited officials from forming factions and introduced the crime of "treacherous cliques," which was not included in previous penal codes.

(3) Severe punishment for officials' crimes of corruption. Emperor Hongwu paid close attention to rectifying the rules of officials, influencing Ming legislation. "Great Admonition of Ming Dynasty" already demonstrated the severity of anti-corruption laws at that time. In the codified "Statutes of Great Ming Dynasty," punishing corrupt officials remained a crucial focus.

(4) Intensify measures against robbery and theft. The law stipulated severe punishments for robbery; even if no property was obtained, the punishment included beating and exile. For anyone who had stolen property, whether as a principal or an accomplice, execution was mandatory. The "Regulations on Griminal Trials" during the Wanli period further specified: "Robbers who murder, set fires, rape, or assault and rob prisons, warehouses, and governmental offices, and those who gather in groups of a hundred or more, will be executed according to the law of robbery, regardless of whether they acquired property." Regarding theft, the Tang Dynasty did not impose the death penalty for theft, but the Ming Dynasty differed: anyone committing theft three times was sentenced to death by hanging.

The Ming Dynasty continued the Tang legal system's five punishments: flogging, beating, penal servitude, exile, and death penalty. "Court beating" was a special punishment used by the Ming emperors to punish ministers, initiated by Emperor Hongwu and commonly used after the reign of Emperor Wuzong. According to *The History of the Ming Dynasty: Records of Penal Law,*in the "Debate over Emperor Wuzong's Southern Tour," the emperor court-beat 146 people in one instance, resulting in 11 deaths. During Emperor Shizong's reign, in the "Great Rites Controversy," 134 officials were beaten, resulting in 16 deaths.

第十课

清朝时期的法律（一）

（课）前准备

图 10-1　辽宁沈阳：清沈阳故宫

　　明朝万历四十四年（1616 年），建州女真首领努尔哈赤建立后金政权，自立为汗，并于 1618 年起兵反明。1636 年，努尔哈赤第八子皇太极称帝，定国号为大清。1644 年，明朝灭亡，清军入关、定鼎北京。这是继蒙元王朝之后由少数民族所建立的又一个统一王朝。至 1912 年清帝逊位，民国创建，清王朝共历经 12 代帝王，享祚 276 年。经康熙初年的稳定与发展，清王朝在康熙、雍正、乾隆三朝形成了持续 130 余年的"康雍乾盛世"。清王朝立足于满汉一体的立国方针，在此基础上形成了其立法指导思想，进行了大量的立法活动。乾隆五年（1740 年）颁行的《钦定大清律例》（通称《大清律例》）是清王朝的代表性法典，其继承了汉、唐以来形成的中华法系法典编纂传统，成为中国历代传世成文法典宝库中的重要一部。[1]

In the 44th year of the Wanli reign of the Ming Dynasty (1616), Nurhachi, the leader of the Jianzhou Jurchens, established the Later Jin regime, proclaimed himself Khan, and launched a military campaign against the Ming Dynasty in 1618. In 1636, Huang Taiji, the eighth son of Nurhaci, ascended the throne as emperor, officially naming the dynasty the "Great Qing." In 1644, with the fall of the Ming Dynasty, the Qing troops marched into the Central Plains and established their capital in Beijing. This marked the second unified dynasty founded by an ethnic minority in Chinese history, following the Mongol Yuan Dynasty. The Qing Dynasty lasted for 276 years, with 12 emperors reigning until 1912, when the last Qing emperor abdicated and the Republic of China was founded. After a period of stabilization and development in the early years of the Kangxi reign, the Qing Dynasty entered the "Kang-Yong-Qian Prosperous Period," which spanned over 130 years through the successive reigns of Kangxi, Yongzheng, and Qianlong. Adopting the governing principle of integrating Manchu and Han peoples, the Qing Dynasty formulated its legislative guiding ideology on this basis and carried out extensive legislative activities. The "Statutes and Regulations of Great Qing Dynasty as Authorized by the Emperor," commonly known as the "Statutes and Regulations of Great Qing Dynasty," promulgated in the fifth year of the Qianlong reign (1740), stands as the representative legal code of the Qing Dynasty. "Statutes and Regulations of Great Qing Dynasty" inherited the tradition of codifying legal codes in the Chinese legal system that had been formed since the Han and Tang Dynasties, and became an important code in the treasure trove of existing written legal codes of successive dynasties in China.

---

〔1〕　参见朱勇主编：《中国法律史》，中国政法大学出版社 2021 年版，第 272~274 页。

生词表

序号	生词	词性	汉语拼音	英文解释
1	定鼎	v.	dìng dǐng	establish the capital
2	逊位	v.	xùn wèi	abdicate
3	享祚	v.	xiǎng zuò	reign over the throne
4	酝酿	v.	yùn niàng	be in the making
5	立足	v.	lì zú	base oneself upon
6	方针	n.	fāng zhēn	guiding principle
7	继承	v.	jì chéng	inherit
8	编纂	v.	biān zuǎn	compile
9	传世	adj.	chuán shì	be handed down from ancient times

导 读

顺治二年（1645 年），清廷设立常设立法机构——律例馆，开始修律工作。次年，修律工作完成，定名《大清律集解附例》，这是清代入关后制定的第一部成文法典。雍正时期，将《大清律集解附例》和康熙朝修成的《现行则例》予以系统编辑，于雍正五年（1727 年）颁行《大清律集解》。乾隆元年（1736 年），清廷对《大清律集解》重新加以考订，此次撰修成果，即乾隆五年颁行的《钦定大清律例》，通称的《大清律例》即指这部法典。[1]

课 文

《钦定大清律例》是清代最为系统同时也是最有代表性的成文法典。该法典在体例上沿袭明律，分为名例、吏、户、礼、兵、刑、工等 7 篇，47 卷 30 门，其内容包括律文 436 条、例文 1409 条、比引律条 30 条。

---

〔1〕 参见朱勇主编：《中国法律史》，中国政法大学出版社 2021 年版，第 274 页。

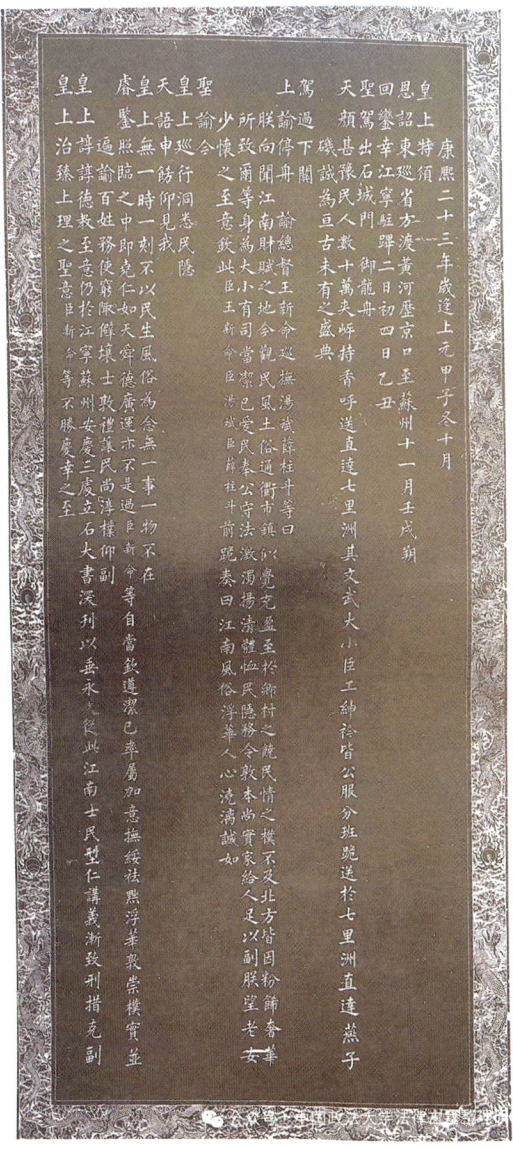

图 10-2　清·《圣谕诫碑》[1]

---

〔1〕　转引自《法制文物日历｜三月四日·清·〈圣谕诫碑〉》，载"中国政法大学法律古籍整理研究所"公众号 2025 年 3 月 4 日，https://mp.weixin.qq.com/s/Uf-erjMPkOVJIqnDmsResA，最后访问日期：2025 年 5 月 30 日。

《钦定大清律例》在编纂条例时，撰修者废除了明朝及清初以时间为序的分类方法，而改为按具体条例的内容与性质分类附入律条，对传统法典编纂方式有所创新，最终完成了律例合体的法典编纂模式，即，将同样性质的条例，分别编在相应律条的后面。这种编排方式下的律例体系，既方便司法者运用，又有助于解决法律施行过程中律例相抵牾的问题。

清代在沿袭明代例典体系的基础上多有创新，特别是在则例制定方面成绩斐然。清代的例，在广义上主要包括条例、则例和事例；狭义上专指条例。

"条例"一词出现于汉代，最早被用于经学研究。南北朝时期，条例开始作为法律用语，首先被运用于礼制领域，作为律条的代称。清代的条例主要用以表示刑事法规，当时人们把《大清律例》中的附例和续纂的刑例称为条例。

"则例"之名起于唐、五代时期，"则"是法则、准则或规则之意，"例"是指先例、成例或定例。到清代，则例的适用范围更为广泛，其法律地位有所提高，成为国家机关运行和重大事务管理的规则。当时不仅有六部则例、各部院则例，中央机构各司制定的各类细则也多以则例为名，则例成为规范清代中央各衙门活动规则的主要法律形式。[1]

"事例"作为法律用语，其确切起源尚不明确。清代在事例的制定方面，基本沿袭了明代的做法。事例是经皇帝裁定、颁布的，作为有司行事规范的某一具体事项或单个的案例，条例即是在事例的基础上编纂的。

在律例关系方面，清代制例的基本要求是*"立例以辅律，贵依律以定例"*[2]，例一方面当与律义相合，另一方面应可补律所不备。清末薛允升把清代律例关系概括为：*"律为一定不易之成法，例为因时制宜之良规。故凡律所不备，必藉有例，以权其小大轻重之衡。使之纤悉比附，归于至当。"*[3]

---

〔1〕 参见杨一凡：《重新认识中国法律史》，社会科学文献出版社 2013 年版，第 297~346 页；王旭：《则例沿革稽考》，中国民主法制出版社 2016 年版，第 37~304 页。

〔2〕 （清）沈家本撰，邓经元、骈宇骞点校：《历代刑法考》（第四册），中华书局 1985 年版，第 2263 页。

〔3〕 （清）薛允升著述，黄静嘉编校：《读例存疑重刊本》（第一册），成文出版社 1970 年版，第 68 页。

生词表

序号	生词	词性	汉语拼音	英文解释
1	抵牾	*v.*	dǐ wǔ	conflict with
2	斐然	*adj.*	fěi rán	brilliant
3	广义	*n.*	guǎng yì	broad sense
4	狭义	*n.*	xiá yì	narrow sense
5	代称	*n.*	dài chēng	another name
6	法规	*n.*	fǎ guī	laws and regulations
7	国家机关	*phr.*	guó jiā jī guān	state organ
8	细则	*n.*	xì zé	detailed rules and regulations
9	衙门	*n.*	yá men	government office in feudal China
10	裁定	*v.*	cái dìng	adjudicate
11	因时制宜	*idm.*	yīn shí zhì yí	use methods appropriate to the current situation

重 点汉字【辟】

图 10-3 "辟"字篆刻（王琦 刻）

辟，汉语一级字。本义是"法"，特指刑法，如："大辟"是中国古代旧五刑之一，隋朝以前是死刑的通称。在古代，君权至上，王命就是王法，所以"君王"也可以被称为"辟"，如"复辟"一词就是指已经失去王位的君王后来又恢复了王位。由执行死刑的含义引申，"辟"又指消除、屏除，如《墨子·尚贤上》："举公义，辟私怨。"

后来词义扩大，"辟"泛指一般的惩罚。有罪者才处刑，故"辟"又引申出"罪"的含义。罪人都被认为是行为不正的人，因此"辟"的含义又引申为邪僻、不正派。

 ## 汉字拓展

序号	词汇	汉语拼音	英文解释	例句
1	征辟	zhēng bì	recruiting and appointing of capable civilians by the court	他因品德高尚被朝廷征辟为御史大夫。
2	复辟	fù bì	restore a monarchy	在那场政变之后，原本被推翻的君主企图复辟旧王朝，但遭到了国内民众的强烈反对。
3	辟邪	bì xié	exorcize evil spirits	人们常常佩戴玉佩或悬挂桃木剑来辟邪。
4	辟易	bì yì	back away in fear	面对那突如其来的巨变，众人无不辟易失色。
5	辟举	bì jǔ	official recruitment and recommendation system	在古代，许多有识之士通过辟举制度，被朝廷直接征召入朝为官。
6	辟谷	bì gǔ	refuse to eat grain	为了修炼身心，他决定进行为期一周的辟谷。
7	百辟	bǎi bì	various feudal lords and high-ranking officials	在盛大的庆典上，百辟云集，共同见证了这一历史性的时刻。

续表

序号	词汇	汉语拼音	英文解释	例句
8	辟聘	pì pìn	invite and appoint	为了吸引顶尖人才，公司决定采取创新的辟聘策略。
9	荐辟	jiàn bì	recommendations and appointments by invitation	在古代，许多才华横溢却出身寒微的士子，通过地方长官的荐辟，得以进入官场。

 化知识【曹雪芹和《红楼梦》】

曹雪芹（约 1715 年 ~1763 年），名霑，字梦阮，号雪芹，是中国清代著名的小说家、文学家。他最为人熟知的是其代表作《红楼梦》。

曹雪芹出身于一个曾经显赫的贵族家庭，其祖上曾是清朝的内务府官员，家庭富裕，因此曹雪芹少年时曾过着纨绔子弟的生活。然而，雍正时期，曹家因多项罪名被抄没家产，曹雪芹在青年时经历了家道中落，晚年生活潦倒贫困，这种生活经历对他创作《红楼梦》产生了深远的影响。《红楼梦》反映了一个家族和整个社会的盛衰兴亡，描绘了许多人物的情感纠葛与命运悲剧。

图 10-4　国家典籍博物馆：清·《脂砚斋重评石头记》

《红楼梦》原名《石头记》，是中国古代文学四大名著之一。全书共 120 回，其中前 80 回由曹雪芹创作，后 40 回则是后人续写的（一般认为由高鹗所续）。《红楼梦》通过对贾、史、王、薛四大家族兴衰历程的描述，展现了封建社会末期贵族家庭的生活，刻画了诸多女性的悲惨命运。小说以贾府为核心，描写了家族内外的种种纷争与情感纠葛，反映了封建社会走向没落的必然趋势。

《红楼梦》围绕贾府的日常生活展开，通过贾宝玉与林黛玉的爱情悲剧，描写家族兴衰的故事，更对当时的社会和人性提出深刻的批判和反思。通过描写贵族家庭的种种情感和冲突，小说揭示了封建社会的虚伪和道德败坏，展现了封建制度下女性的悲剧命运。

《红楼梦》以其细腻的心理描写、丰富的人物塑造和深刻的社会批判，被誉为中国古典小说的巅峰之作。曹雪芹在创作中采用了"梦境"与"现实"相结合的叙事手法，语言生动，使所呈现的人物性格鲜明。他对封建社会的深刻批判，对人性和情感的细腻描绘，使《红楼梦》成为中国文学史上独具一格的杰出作品。

（法）治文物【日晷】

图 10-5　日晷[1]

----

〔1〕 参见《清·日晷》，载中国政法大学中华法制文明虚拟博物馆，https://flgj.cupl.edu.cn/info/1072/1676.htm，最后访问日期：2024 年 12 月 9 日。

日晷，清代计时器。北京紫禁城中重要宫殿前面均置有日晷，即除午门、太和殿、乾清宫、坤宁宫外，东北方向的皇极殿、养性殿、颐和轩，西侧的养心殿、慈宁宫等建筑物前均有石质日晷。日晷由圆形晷盘和一根铜制晷针组成，盘双面均刻划有 12 个时辰，利用日光照射指针在晷盘上的投影标示时间。春分开始观测太阳在上盘面的投影，秋分开始观测太阳在下盘面的投影。记天时、行历法是国家重要的政务，因此以日晷为标志"授时行历"也是统治天下的一种手段，蕴藏着不可忤逆的政治信念。

经 典阅读

图 10-6　国家典籍博物馆:《红楼梦》萃文书屋活字印本

《红楼梦》第三回：贾雨村夤缘复旧职　林黛玉抛父进京都（节选）

贾母因笑道："外客未见，就脱了衣裳，还不去见你妹妹！"宝玉早已看见多了一个姊妹，便料定是林姑妈之女，忙来作揖。厮见毕归坐，细看形容，与众各别：两弯似蹙非蹙罥烟眉，一双似喜非喜含情目。态生两靥之愁，娇袭一身之病。泪光点点，娇喘微微。闲静时如姣花照水，行动处似弱柳扶风。心较比干多一窍，病如西子胜三分。

宝玉看罢，因笑道："这个妹妹我曾见过的。"贾母笑道："可又是胡说，你又何曾见过他？"宝玉笑道："虽然未曾见过他，然我看着面善，心里就算是旧相识，今日只作远别重逢，亦未为不可。"贾母笑道："更好，更好，若如此，更相和睦了。"宝玉便走近黛玉身边坐下，又细细打量一番，因问："妹妹可曾读书？"黛玉道："不曾读，只上了一年学，些须认得几个字。"宝玉又道："妹妹尊名是那两个字？"黛玉便说了名。宝玉又问表字。黛玉道："无字。"宝玉笑道："我送妹妹一妙字，莫若'颦颦'二字极妙。"探春便问何出。宝玉道："《古今人物通考》上说：'西方有石名黛，可代画眉之墨。'况这林妹妹眉尖若蹙，用取这两个字，岂不两妙！"探春笑道："只恐又是你的杜撰。"宝玉笑道："除《四书》外，杜撰的太多，偏只我是杜撰不成？"又问黛玉："可也有玉没有？"众人不解其语，黛玉便忖度着因他有玉，故问我有也无，因答道："我没有那个。想来那玉是一件罕物，岂能人人有的。"

宝玉听了，登时发作起痴狂病来，摘下那玉，就狠命摔去，骂道："什么罕物，连人之高低不择，还说'通灵'不'通灵'呢！我也不要这劳什子了！"吓的众人一拥争去拾玉。贾母急的搂了宝玉道："孽障！你生气，要打骂人容易，何苦摔那命根子！"宝玉满面泪痕泣道："家里姐姐妹妹都没有，单我有，我说没趣；如今来了这么一个神仙似的妹妹也没有，可知这不是个好东西。"贾母忙哄他道："你这妹妹原有这个来的，因你姑妈去世时，舍不得你妹妹，无法处，遂将他的玉带了去了：一则全殉葬之礼，尽你妹妹之孝心；二则你姑妈之灵，亦可权作见了女儿之意。因此他只说没有这个，不便自己夸张之意。你如今怎比得他？还不好生慎重带上，仔细你娘知道了。"说着，便向丫鬟手中接来，亲与他带上。宝玉听如此说，想一想大有情理，也就不生别论了。

 参考译文

Grandmother Jia smiled and said, "You haven't greeted our guest yet, and you've already taken off your clothes. Go and meet your sister!" Baoyu had already noticed there was an additional sister and guessed that she was mostly like the daughter of Aunt Lin, so he quickly came forward to greet her. After the greetings, they returned to their seats. Baoyu scrutinized her appearance and found her quite different from the others: Her eyebrows were like misty smoke, neither fully furrowed nor smooth, and her eyes seemed to hold both joyful yet not, brimming with affection. Her face bore a natural melancholy, showing on her dimples, and her delicate figure seemed to be afflicted by illness. Her eyes glistened with tears, and her breathing was slightly labored. When she was still, she was like a beautiful flower reflecting in the water; when she moved, she was like a delicate willow swaying in the wind. Her heart was more intelligent and sensitive than Bi Gan's, and her sickly charm surpassed that of Xi Shi.

After looking her over, Baoyu smiled and said, "I've seen this sister before." Grandmother Jia chuckled and said, "You're talking nonsense again. When have you ever seen her?" Baoyu smiled and replied, "Although I haven't seen her before, she looks familiar to me. In my heart, we're old acquaintances. It wouldn't be inappropriate to consider today as a reunion after a long separation." Grandmother Jia smiled and said, "Even better. If that's the case, you'll get along even more harmoniously." Baoyu then approached Daiyu and sat down beside her, scrutinizing her once more. He asked, "Has sister studied any books?" Daiyu replied, "No, I only attended school for a year and can recognize a few characters." Baoyu then asked, "What is sister's given name?" Daiyu told him. Baoyu then inquired about her style name, and Daiyu said, "I don't have one." Baoyu smiled and said, "I'll give sister a wonderful style name. How about 'Pinpin'? It's perfect." Tanchun asked where it came from, and Baoyu explained, "*The Comprehensive Examination of Ancient and Modern Figures* says, 'In the West, there is a stone called Dai, which can be used as ink for painting eyebrows.' Since this younger sister's eyebrows are slightly furrowed, using these two characters would be doubly wonderful!" Tanchun chuckled and said, "I'm afraid it's just your invention again." Baoyu laughed and said, "Apart from the Four Books, there are too many inventions. Why can't I be the one to invent something?" He then asked Daiyu, "Do you also have a jade pendant?" The others didn't understand what he meant, but Daiyu guessed that he was asking because he had a jade pendant and wanted to know if she had one too. She replied, "I don't have that. I suppose that jade pendant is a rare object, not something everyone can have."

Upon hearing this, Baoyu suddenly became furious and snatched off his jade pendant, violently throwing it to the ground and cursing, "What kind of rare object is this? It doesn't even distinguish between people of high and low status. It claims to be 'spiritual,' but is it really? I don't want this thing anymore!" Everyone was frightened and rushed to pick up the jade pendant. Grandmother Jia hurriedly hugged Baoyu and said, "You wretch! It's easy to get angry and scold people, but why do you have to throw away your lifeline?" Baoyu wept with tears streaming down his face and said, "None of my sisters at home have this jade pendant, only I do. I find it dull. Now, even such a fairy-like sister has none. Clearly, this isn't a good thing." Grandmother Jia hurriedly soothed him, saying, "Your sister originally had this jade pendant. When your aunt passed away, she couldn't bear to part with your sister and had no other choice but to take it with her: firstly, to fulfill the ritual of burial and show your sister's filial piety; secondly, your aunt's spirit could also be considered as having seen her daughter again. That's why she only said she didn't have it, not wanting to boast about it. How can you compare yourself to her? You should carefully wear it again. Be careful that your mother finds out." Saying this, she took the jade pendant from the maid's hand and put it on Baoyu herself. After hearing this, Baoyu thought it made sense and didn't argue anymore.

课 后练习

1. 选择题：清代最为系统同时也是最有代表性的成文法典是（　　）。
A.《大清律集解附例》
B.《现行则例》

C.《大清律集解》

D.《钦定大清律例》

2.判断题：清代的例，在广义上专指条例。

3.填空题：《钦定大清律例》在编纂条例时，撰修者废除了明朝及清初以_____为序的分类方法，而改为按_____分类附入律条，对传统法典编纂方式有所创新，最终完成了律例合体的法典编纂模式。

4.简答题：解释"条例""则例""事例"的含义及其在清代的制定情况。

5.讨论题：清朝的律例关系以及律例在司法审判中各自的作用。

课 文参考翻译

"Statutes and Regulations of Great Qing Dynasty as Authorized by the Emperor" is the most systematic and representative codified law of the Qing Dynasty. The code follows the style and structure of the Ming law, divided into 7 sections, Names and Examples, Personnel, Revenue, Rites, War, Punishments, and Works. It consists of 47 volumes, 30 categories, and the content of which includes 436 statutes, 1409 regulations, and 30 comparative reference articles.

When compiling the regulations of "Statutes and Regulations of Great Qing Dynasty as Authorized by the Emperor," the compilers abolished the classification method of the Ming Dynasty and the early Qing Dynasty which was in chronological order. Instead, they changed to classify the content and nature of the specific regulations, and attach them to the relevant statutes. This was an innovation in the traditional codification method, and finally completed the codification mode of the combination of the statutes and regulations, that is, to compile the regulations of the same nature respectively behind the corresponding statutes. This arrangement in the system of laws and regulations not only facilitates the use by the judiciary, but also helps to solve the problem of contradictory statutes and regulations in the process of law enforcement.

The Qing Dynasty, on the basis of inheriting the system of the Ming Dynasty, made many new innovations, especially achieving remarkable success in the formulation of regulatory statutes. In the Qing Dynasty, regulations, in a broad sense, mainly included 条例（regulations）、则例（regulations and precedents）, and 事例（case regulations）; in a narrow sense, they specifically referred to 条例（regulations）.

The term 条例（regulations）appeared in the Han Dynasty and was first used in the study of Confucian classics. During the Northern and Southern Dynasties, the term began to be used as a legal term and was first applied to the field of etiquette, serving as a substitute for legal provisions. In the Qing Dynasty, although it followed the system of the Ming system, there were also some changes. The regulations in the Qing Dynasty were mainly used to denote criminal law. At that time, people referred to the supplementary regulations in the "Statutes and Regulations of Great Qing Dynasty" and the newly compiled criminal regulations as "条例（regulations）."

The term 则例（regulations and precedents）originated in the Tang Dynasty and the period of the Five Dynasties. 则（regulations）means laws, guidelines or rules, while 例 refers to precedents, established practices or fixed examples. In the Qing Dynasty, the scope of application of regulations and precedents was much broader, and their legal status was enhanced, becoming the rules for the operation of state organs and the management of major affairs. At that time, there were not only the regulations and precedents of the Six Ministries and those of various government departments and courts. Moreover, various detailed rules formulated by different divisions of the central institutions were also mostly named as regulations and precedents. They became the main form of law regulated the activities of various central government departments in the Qing Dynasty.

As a legal term, the exact origin of 事例（case regulations）is not clear. In the Qing Dynasty, the practice of formulating cases basically followed that of the Ming Dynasty. Case regulations are determined and promulgated by the emperor. They serve as the norms for relevant departments to act in a specific matter or as a single case. Regulations are compiled on the basis of these case regulations.

In the relationship between 律（statutes）and 例（regulations）in the Qing Dynasty, the basic requirement for formulating regulations was to "establish regulations to supplement the statutes, and it is important to determine the regulations in accordance with the statutes." On the one hand, the regulations should be consistent with the meaning of the statutes, and on the other hand, they should be able to make up for what the statutes fail to cover. At the end of the Qing Dynasty, Xue Yunsheng summarized the relationship between the statutes and regulations of the Qing Dynasty as follows: "Statutes are established and unchangeable laws that cannot be easily altered, while regulations are good norms formulated according to different times to adapt to the actual situations. Therefore, whenever there are aspects not elaborated in the statutes, it is necessary to rely on the regulations to weigh the magnitude and severity of matters. This enables all details to be applied appropriately and fittingly, ultimately achieving the most appropriate and reasonable state."

第十一课

清朝时期的法律（二）

（课）前准备

图 11-1　国家典籍博物馆：《耕织图》清乾隆刻套印本

　　强调天人合一观念是清朝司法思想的特色之一。天人合一是古代中国的重要思想观念，是政治、法律的合理性依据之一。俗语云："人命关天"，即是天人合一思想在司法领域的重要体现。清代君主多以此训诲臣下重视刑狱之事，以免招致上天责罚。《礼记·月令》即有对于"秋冬行刑"的记载，董仲舒在他"春秋大一统"的理论框架中对此做了更体系化的论证：**"庆赏罚刑，与春夏秋冬以类相应也……天有四时，王有四政"**，故圣王应春夏行赏，秋冬行刑。如刑赏失时，则会招致灾祸，受到上天惩罚。"秋冬行刑"的思想影响到制度建设层面，在清代就出现了秋审制度，秋审制度是在天人合一思想影响下极度慎重对待民命理念的制度设计。[1]

Emphasizing the concept of the unity of heaven and man is one of the characteristics of the Qing judicial thought. The unity of man and heaven is an important ideological concept in ancient China, which is one of the rational bases of politics and law. As the saying goes, "Human life is a matter of heaven ." This is an important embodiment of the idea of the unity of

---

　　[1]　参见朱勇主编：《中国法律史》，中国政法大学出版社 2021 年版，第 285~287 页。

heaven and man in the judicial field. The monarchs of the Qing Dynasty often taught their subordinates to pay attention to criminal cases, so as to avoid incurring heavenly chastisement. *The Book of Rites*: *Monthly Orders* has a record of "execution in autumn and winter," and Dong Zhongshu made a more systematic argument within his theoretical framework of "Grand Unification in the Spring and Autumn Annals"： "Celebrations, rewards, and punishments, which are part of the four administrative measures, correspond to spring, summer, autumn, and winter...There are four seasons in heaven, and four administrations for the king." So the sage king should grant rewards in spring and summer and carry out executions in autumn and winter. If the punishment and reward are out of time, they will lead to disasters and bring about punishment from heaven. The idea of "execution in autumn and winter" affects the institutional construction. The Autumn Trial system emerged in the Qing Dynasty. The Autumn Trial system is a system design that reflects the concept of treating people's lives with extreme caution under the influence of the idea of the unity of heaven and man.

 生词表

序号	生词	词性	汉语拼音	英文解释
1	天人合一	*idm.*	tiān rén hé yī	the unity of heaven and man, as human beings are an integral part of nature
2	观念	*n.*	guān niàn	concept
3	依据	*n.*	yī jù	basis
4	云	*v.*	yún	say，express
5	人命关天	*idm.*	rén mìng guān tiān	human life is a matter of heaven, as human life is of crucial importance
6	训诲	*v.*	xùn huì	instruct
7	招致	*v.*	zhāo zhì	bring about
8	责罚	*v.*	zé fá	punish

续表

序号	生词	词性	汉语拼音	英文解释
9	春秋大一统	*phr.*	chūn qiū dà yī tǒng	the idea of achieving overall unity in various aspects during the Spring and Autumn Period in ancient China
10	框架	*n.*	kuàng jià	framework
11	体系化	*adj.*	tǐ xì huà	systematic
12	论证	*v.*	lùn zhèng	expound and prove
13	灾祸	*n.*	zāi huò	disaster
14	慎重	*adj.*	shèn zhòng	prudent

 **导 读**

　　清代将死刑犯人分为立决和监候两种。立决就是立即执行（重罪立即处决又分凌迟、斩立决、绞立决）；监候则为缓决（罪行较轻或案情可疑的判为斩监候、绞监候），等待当年秋审再决定是否执行死刑。此前，死罪尚无立决、监候之别，明孝宗弘治十年（1497 年）始有此区别，至《大清律》成为法定制度。清朝所有死刑案件，经"三法司"复核，内阁票拟或军机大臣会商拟办后，须请示皇帝加以裁决。经皇帝决定为监候的案件，即进入秋审程序。[1]

课 文

　　秋审是针对已判处斩、绞监候的案件，由三法司每年一度在全国范围内进行复核的制度。秋审最主要的工作就是把在押监候死囚分为"实、缓、矜、留"四项："情实"，案情属实、罪名适当，可执行死刑；"缓决"，罪行较轻，继续监候，留待下年秋审再行复核；"可矜"，罪行属实，但情有可原者，可减等免死发落；"留养承祀"，按照法律本无可饶恕的重罪犯人，如果是独子而父母又年老多病无人奉养，可特别恩准免死。在实际审判结果中，"矜""留"

---

〔1〕　参见朱勇主编：《中国法律史》，中国政法大学出版社 2021 年版，第 292 页。

两类情况较少。

图 11-2　清·《十万图·万丈空流》（任熊）

秋审的主要程序包括：①初审：对各省奏报的秋审题本，先由刑部审录，摘叙案件缘由，写出具体结论。②会审与题报：由大学士、九卿、詹事、科道等在京三品以上官员齐集一起，进行会审，然后由刑部分情实、缓决、可矜、留养承祀四本向皇帝题报。③皇帝批示：奉旨缓决、可矜、留养承祀的案犯其秋审程序即告结束，奉旨情实者，仍要复奏。④复奏和勾决：死刑执行前复审官员向皇帝复奏，以示特别慎重。复奏本上，由皇帝用朱笔在应立决案犯名上打勾，称为"勾决"，表示一旦勾到，即行处决。

清代皇帝非常重视秋审。在勾决前，皇帝会斋戒；勾决之时，皇帝和秋审官员皆素服，一般由皇帝在复奏本的死囚名字旁划勾，最后还要在复奏本前几页用红笔把勾决的名字抄录一遍，以免误勾，昭示慎重。

因之前的各级审理已严格按照法律规定进行，故秋审就不再是一种简单的法律审查，而是根据特定的时势，注重政策的调整，力争在综合天理、国法和人情的基础上作出最妥当的判决。秋审制度使死刑复核被纳入了前所未有的严格的法律程序中，保证了皇帝对死刑的控制权，在全国范围内最大可能地做到了司法的统一，控制了地方各自为政和擅杀滥杀的风险。据统计，大致有 3/4 的死刑监候犯人，在经历一次或若干次秋审后，被免于死刑处罚。[1]

 生词表

序号	生词	词性	汉语拼音	英文解释
1	监候	*n.*	jiān hòu	awaiting execution under surveillance
2	案件	*n.*	àn jiàn	case
3	三法司	*proper n.*	Sān fǎ sī	the Ministry of Punishments，the Court of Judicial Review and the Censorate as the Three Judicial Departments in the Ming and Qing Dynasties
4	复核	*v.*	fù hé	review
5	判处	*v.*	pàn chǔ	sentence
6	奏报	*v.*	zòu bào	memorialize the emperor
7	题本	*n.*	tí běn	memorial on autumn assize
8	审录	*v.*	shěn lù	examine and record
9	摘叙	*v.*	zhāi xù	excerpt and narrate
10	批示	*v.*	pī shì	write comments or instructions
11	奉旨	*adv.*	fèng zhǐ	be at the emperor's order
12	案犯	*n.*	àn fàn	criminal
13	斋戒	*v.*	zhāi jiè	fast
14	素服	*n.*	sù fú	white mourning clothes
15	昭示	*v.*	zhāo shì	make clear to all

---

〔1〕 参见孙家红：《视野放宽：对清代秋审和朝审结果的新考察》，载《清史研究》2007 年第 3 期。

续表

序号	生词	词性	汉语拼音	英文解释
16	时势	*n.*	shí shì	the current situation
17	判决	*n.*	pàn jué	pronounce judgement
18	擅杀	*v.*	shàn shā	kill without authorization
19	滥杀	*v.*	làn shā	kill indiscriminately

重 点汉字【笞】

图 11-3　"笞"字篆刻 （王琦 刻）

笞，汉语二级字。本义指用竹板、荆条击打，后指古代用竹板、荆条或其他工具殴打人的脊背或臀腿的刑罚，如封建五刑中的"笞刑"。

 汉字拓展

序号	词汇	汉语拼音	英文解释	例句
1	鞭笞	biān chī	flog	作家在小说中鞭笞了丑恶的社会现象。
2	笞罚	chī fá	flogging penalty	在古代社会，对于违反法律或社会规范的行为，有时会采取笞罚作为惩罚手段。

续表

序号	词汇	汉语拼音	英文解释	例句
3	搒笞	péng chī	torture	在那个时代，即便是轻微的过错也可能招致搒笞，以致人们生活在恐惧之中。
4	笞戮	chī lù	flog and kill	在那段动荡不安的岁月里，暴虐的统治者视人命如草芥，稍有不顺其意者，便可能遭受笞戮的极刑。
5	笞杀	chī shā	flog to death	在古代，有些正直之士因坚守正义，得罪奸佞而被笞杀。
6	笞叱	chī chì	beat and scold	古代军纪严苛，违纪士兵常被当众笞叱。

文 化知识【吴敬梓和《儒林外史》】

图11-4　山东青州：一门科第坊

《儒林外史》是清代作家吴敬梓创作的一部卓越的长篇小说，这部作品以写实主义手法，揭露了封建社会中官场的黑暗、科举制度对人性的腐蚀以及虚伪欺诈的社会风气，被誉为中国古代讽刺小说的高峰。全书共 56 回，没有贯穿全书的中心人物或主要情节，而是由众多相对独立的故事连缀而成，通过一系列生动的儒林人物形象，展现了普通士人日常生活的生存状态与精神追求。《儒林外史》的讽刺艺术高超，通过寓言式的故事和夸张的手法，对当时社会的种种弊端进行了深刻的批判和嘲讽，同时，小说也热情地歌颂了少数人物以坚持自我的方式所作的对于人性的守护，寄寓了作者的理想信念。

法　治文物【仿新莽嘉量】

图 11-5　仿新莽嘉量[1]

　　在北京故宫太和殿与乾清宫前的丹陛之上各陈设有一件铜制镀金嘉

---

　　〔1〕　参见《清·仿新莽嘉量》，载中国政法大学中华法制文明虚拟博物馆，https://flgj.cupl.edu.cn/info/1072/1659.htm，最后访问日期：2024 年 12 月 4 日。

量——它们由汉白玉石亭妥善围护，是清代重要的礼器。这两件嘉量形制的核心母本，正是历史上著名的新莽铜嘉量（即"王莽嘉量"）。

作为中国古代度量衡的标志性器物，王莽嘉量看似是单一器具，实则是一套精密的组合量器：它将斛、斗、升、合、龠五种容量单位整合为一体，且明确规定了单位换算关系——二龠为合，十合为升，十升为斗，十斗为斛。更精妙的是，王莽嘉量每个量器的器身上都详细铭刻了自身的直径、深度、底面积及容积数据，因此其不仅是实用的测量工具，更是新莽政权确立的国家法定标准量器。

乾隆时期仿制的这两件嘉量，虽以王莽嘉量为母本，却承载了清代独特的政治象征意义：它们"列于大庭"（置于太和殿、乾清宫等核心宫殿前），既是对古代度量衡传统的承袭，更成为清帝国"法制一统"的具象符号——通过标准化的象征器物，彰显国家度量、制度的统一权威。

经典阅读

《儒林外史》第三回：周学道校士拔真才　胡屠户行凶闹捷报（节选）

到出榜那日，家里没有早饭的米，母亲吩咐范进道："我有一只生蛋的母鸡，你快拿集上去卖了，买几升米来煮餐粥吃，我已是饿的两眼都看不见了。"范进慌忙抱了鸡，走出门去。才去不到两个时候，只听得一片声的锣响，三匹马闯将来。那三个人下了马，把马拴在茅草棚上，一片声叫道："快请范老爷出来，恭喜高中了！"母亲不知是甚事，吓得躲在屋里；听见中了，方敢伸出头来，说道："诸位请坐，小儿方才出去了。"那些报录人道："原来是老太太。"大家簇拥着要喜钱。正在吵闹，又是几匹马，二报、三报到了，挤了一屋的人，茅草棚地下都坐满了。邻居都来了，挤着看。老太太没奈何，只得央及一个邻居去寻他儿子。

那邻居飞奔到集上，一地里寻不见，直寻到集东头，见范进抱着鸡，手里插个草标，一步一踱的东张西望，在那里寻人买。邻居道："范相公，快些回去！你恭喜中了举人，报喜人挤了一屋里。"范进当是哄他，只装不听见，低着头往前走。邻居见他不理，走上来，就要夺他手里的鸡。范进道："你夺我的鸡怎的？你又不买。"邻居道："你中了举了，叫你家去打发报子哩。"范进道："高邻，你晓得我今日没有米，要卖这鸡去救命，为甚么拿这话来混我？我又不同你顽，你自回去罢，莫误了我卖鸡。"邻居见他不信，劈手把鸡夺了，掼在地下，一把拉了回来。报录人见了道："好了，新贵人回来了。"正要拥着他说话，范进三两步走进屋里来，见中间报帖已经升挂起来，上写道："捷报贵府老爷范讳进高中广东乡试第七名亚元。京报连登黄甲。"

范进不看便罢，看了一遍，又念一遍，自己把两手拍了一下，笑了一声，道："噫！好了！我中了！"说着，往后一跤跌倒，牙关咬紧，不省人事。老太太慌了，慌将几口开水灌了过来。他爬将起来，又拍着手大笑道："噫！好！我中了！"笑着，不由分说就往门外飞跑，把报录人和邻居都吓了一跳。走出大门不多路，一脚踹在塘里，挣起来，头发都跌散了，两手黄泥，淋淋漓漓一身的水。众人拉他不住，拍着笑着，一直走到集上去了。众人大眼望小眼，一齐道："原来新贵人欢喜疯了。"老太太哭道："怎生这样苦命的事！中了一个甚么举人，就得了这个拙病！这一疯了，几时才得好？"娘子胡氏道："早上好好出去，怎的就得了这样的病！却是如何是好？"众邻居劝道："老太太不要心慌。我们而今且派两个人跟定了范老爷。这里众人家里拿些鸡蛋酒米，且管待了报子上的老爹们，再为商酌。"

参考译文

On the day when the list was released, the family did not have rice for breakfast. The mother instructed Fan Jin, saying: "I still have an egg-laying hen. You should quickly take it to the market and sell it, then buy a few liters of rice to cook porridge. I'm already so hungry that I can hardly see anything." Fan Jin hurriedly held the chicken and went out. He had only been gone for less than four hours when he heard the sound of a gong and three men on horseback burst in. The three men dismounted, tied their horses to a thatched hut, and called out repeatedly, "Quickly ask Master Fan to come out, congratulations on passing the provincial level imperial examination!" The mother did not know what had happened and was so frightened that she hid in the house; only when she heard that Fan Jin had been successful in the examination did she dare to stick out her head and explain, "Please sit down, gentlemen; my son has just gone out." The messengers who brought the good news said, "So it's the old lady." They all flocked around, asking for the reward money for delivering the good news. While they were making a lot of noise, a few more men on horseback arrived, bringing the second and third rounds of good news announcements, crowding the room with people, and even the floor of the thatched hut was full. Neighbors also came, crowded around to see the fun. The old lady had no choice but to beg a neighbor to go and find Fan Jin.

The neighbor dashed to the marketplace and could not find him anywhere; it was only when he reached the east side of the marketplace that he saw Fan Jin holding a chicken with a straw marker in his hand, walking slowly and looking around, searching for a buyer there. The neighbor said, "Fan Jin, go back quickly! Congratulations on becoming a successful candidate in the pronvincial imperial examination. The messengers who brought the good news have crowded into your house." Fan Jin thought he was being tricked, so he pretended not to hear and walked on with his head down. The neighbor, seeing that he was ignoring him, came forward and tried to grab the chicken in his hand. Fan Jin said, "What are you doing snatching my chicken? You don't want to buy it." The neighbor said, "You've been successful in the provincial imperial examination, so I'm telling you to go home and deal with those messengers who brought the good news." Fan Jin said, "My dear neighbor, you know that I have no rice for today's meal and I have to sell this chicken to make a living. Why did you lie to me with these words? I'm not going to joke around with you. Go back by yourself, don't delay me in selling the chicken." When the neighbor saw that he did not believe him, he snatched the chicken with one hand, threw it on the ground, and pulled Fan Jin back. When the messengers who brought the good news saw him, they said, "Great, the new nobleman has returned." As they surrounded him to talk, Fan Jin walked quickly into the house in two or three steps and saw that the congratulatory notice in the middle of the house had already been hung up, which read: "Pleased to report that your master Fan Jin ranked seventh among the successful candidates in the Guangdong provincial imperial examination. May your achievements continue to be celebrated as recorded in the official reports from the capital."

Fan Jin would have been better off not looking at it. After looking at it once, he read it again. He clapped his own hands and let out a laugh, saying: "Aha! Great! I've passed the provincial imperial examination!" As he said this, he fell backward in a stumble, his teeth clenched tightly, and lost consciousness. The old lady panicked and quickly poured several mouthfuls of boiled water into his mouth. He got up, clapped his hands again and laughed loudly, saying, "Aha! Great! I've passed the provincial imperial examination!" Still laughing, without waiting for anyone to say anything, he dashed out of the door, startling both the messengers and the neighbors. He hadn't walked far from the main gate when he tripped and fell into a pond. When he struggled to his feet, his hair was all disheveled, his hands were covered in yellow mud, and his whole body was dripping wet. The people around couldn't hold him back. Still clapping his hands and laughing, he walked all the way to the marketplace. All the people stared at each other in surprise and all said, "The new nobleman has gone crazy with joy." The old lady cried: "How could such a pitiful thing happen! Just because he became a successful candidate in the provincial imperial examination, he got this strange illness! Once he's gone crazy like this, when will he get better?" His wife, Mrs. Hu said, "He went out in good health in the morning. How could he suddenly get such an illness? What on earth should we do?" The neighbors tried to console the old lady, saying, "Don't be worried, old lady. For now, let's send two people to keep an eye on Master Fan. Everyone here should bring some eggs, wine and rice from their homes to entertain the messengers, and then we can discuss what to do next."

课 后练习

1. 多选题：以下属于清代死刑中立决的是（　　　）。

A. 凌迟

B. 斩立决

C. 绞立决

D. 监候

2. 判断题：秋审针对的是已判处斩、绞监候的案件。

3. 填空题：_____，案情属实、罪名适当，可执行死刑；_____，罪行较轻，继续监候，留待下年秋审再行复核；_____，罪行属实，但情有可原者，可减等免死发落；_____，按照法律本无可饶恕的重罪犯人，如果是独子而父母又年老多病无人奉养，可特别恩准免死。

4. 简答题：简述清代秋审的四个主要程序及清代皇帝对待秋审的态度。

5. 讨论题：从天理、国法、人情等方面讨论清代秋审制度的意义。

课 文参考翻译

Autumn Trial is for cases where the criminals have been sentenced to death by beheading or death by hanging with a stay of execution. It is a system in which the Three Judicial Departments conduct a nationwide review once a year on these cases of death sentences with a stay of execution. The main work of the Autumn Trial is to divide the death row prisoners who are detained in prison and awaiting execution into four categories: "实 (True Guilt), 缓 (Reprieve), 矜 (Merciful Case), 留 (Permitted to Stay Home to Support Parents and Carry on the Family Line)". For "True Guilt," if the facts of the case are true and the charge is appropriate, the death penalty can be carried out. For "Reprieve," if the crime is relatively minor, the prisoner will continue to be in custody and await the review in the next Autumn Trial. For

"Merciful Case," if the crime is confirmed but there are extenuating circumstances, the punishment can be reduced and the death penalty can be commuted. As for "Permitted to Stay Home to Support Parents and Carry on the Family Line," even though a serious criminal who has committed a crime punishable by beheading or hanging may not deserve leniency according to the law, if they are the only child and their parents are old and ill with no one to take care of them, they can be specially granted exemption from the death penalty. In the actual trial results, cases of the "Merciful Case" and "Permitted to Stay Home to Support Parents and Carry on the Family Line" types are relatively rare.

The main procedures of the Autumn Trial include: ① Preliminary Hearing: For the memorials regarding the Autumn Trial reported by various provinces, the Ministry of Punishment first examines and records them, briefly describes the original reasons of the cases, and writes down specific conclusions. ② Joint Trial and Submission of Memorials: High-ranking officials in the capital such as Grand Secretaries, the Nine Ministers, the Supervisors of the Imperial Academy, and the Censors who hold the rank of third grade or above gather together for a joint trial. Then, led by the Ministry of Punishment, they categorize the cases into four types: "True Guilt," "Reprieve," "Merciful Case," and "Permitted to Stay Home to Support Parents and Carry on the Family Line" and submit memorials to the Emperor. ③ Imperial Approval: For the criminals in the cases of "Reprieve," "Merciful Case," and "Permitted to Stay Home to Support Parents and Carry on the Family Line" approved by the Emperor's decree, the Autumn Trial procedures for them are completed. For those approved as "True Guilt," a re-submission is still required. ④ Re-submission and Verdict Execution: Before the execution of the death penalty, the reviewing officials submit a re-submission to the Emperor to demonstrate special prudence. On the re-submission memorial, the Emperor uses a vermilion brush to put a tick beside the names of the criminals who should be immediately executed. This is called "Hook Decision," which means that once a name is ticked, the execution will be carried out immediately.

Emperors of the Qing Dynasty attached great importance to the Autumn Trial. Before the "Hook Decision" process, the emperor would observe a fast. When making the "Hook Decision," both the emperor and the officials involved in the Autumn Trial would wear white mourning clothes. Generally, the emperor would put a tick beside the names of the death row prisoners on the re-submission memorial. Finally, the officials would also use a vermilion brush to copy the names of those who had been marked for execution on the first few pages of the re-submission memorial, in order to avoid mistakenly marking a name and to demonstrate the solemnity of the process.

Because the previous trials at all levels were conducted in strict accordance with the provisions of the law, the Autumn Trial is no longer a simple legal review. Instead, based on a particular situation, it focuses on policy adjustments and strives to make the most appropriate judgment by integrating the principles of heavenly justice, national laws, and human feelings. The Autumn Trial system has incorporated the review of the death penalty into an unprecedentedly strict legal procedure, ensured the emperor's control over the death penalty, maximized the possibility of achieving judicial unity across the country, and restricted local authorities from acting independently and engaging in arbitrary and indiscriminate executions. According to statistics, roughly three quarters of the prisoners awaiting execution of the death penalty were exempted from the death penalty after one or several Autumn Trials.

清朝时期的法律（三）

课 前准备

图 12-1　故宫博物院：《圆明园铜版画·海晏堂西面》

鸦片战争后，中国受到列强直接的、巨大的冲击，开始了艰难的近代化历程。近代化最开始在军事、国防、经济等领域发生，到戊戌维新前后，其重心开始转移到政法领域。自庚子国变后到清朝灭亡这十余年间，清廷进行了法制改革。这次法制改革是中国传统法制向近代法制转型所迈出的关键一步，具有承前启后、继往开来之地位。在清末，于法律上承先启后、媒介中西法律从而为中国法律的近代化奠定基础者，当首推法律改革的主持者沈家本。[1]

After the Opium War, China was directly and severely impacted by the imperialist powers and embarked on a difficult process of modernization. Modernization initially took place in areas such as military affairs, national defense, and the economy. Around the time of the Hundred Days' Reform, its focus began to shift to the fields of politics and law. From the time of the

---

〔1〕 参见朱勇主编：《中国法律史》，中国政法大学出版社 2021 年版，第 297 页。

Boxer Indemnity Incident (Gengzi Incident) to the fall of the Qing Dynasty, which spanned over a decade, the Qing government carried out legal system reforms. This legal reform was a crucial step in the transformation of China's traditional legal system into a modern one, playing a significant role in connecting the past and the future. At the end of the Qing Dynasty, Shen Jiaben, the person in charge of the legal reforms, was the one who first laid the foundation for the modernization of Chinese law. He inherited the legal traditions of the past and served as a bridge between Chinese and Western laws.

 生词表

序号	生词	词性	汉语拼音	英文解释
1	鸦片战争	*proper n.*	Yā piàn Zhàn zhēng	the war of aggression against China lunched by Britain
2	列强	*n.*	liè qiáng	great powers
3	冲击	*n.*	chōng jī	impact
4	国防	*n.*	guó fáng	national defence
5	领域	*n.*	lǐng yù	field
6	戊戌维新	*proper n.*	Wù xū Wéi xīn	the bourgeois reform movement in the late Qing Dynasty
7	庚子国变	*proper n.*	Gēng zǐ Guó biàn	the crisis year of 1900 involving the Boxer uprising and the eight nation military invasion
8	转型	*v.*	zhuǎn xíng	transform
9	关键	*adj.*	guān jiàn	crucial
10	承前启后 承先启后	*idm.*	chéng qián qǐ hòu chéng xiān qǐ hòu	carry on the past and usher in the future
11	继往开来	*idm.*	jì wǎng kāi lái	carry a cause forward and forge ahead into the future
12	媒介	*v.*	méi jiè	mediate
13	首推	*v.*	shǒu tuī	recommend first

导 读

沈家本（1840 年~1913 年），清末著名的律学家和法学专家。沈家本既是中国传统法制研究的集大成者，也是近代法律体系的奠基人，堪称中国法律近代化的巨擘。1901 年至 1911 年，他历任清王朝刑部侍郎、修订法律大臣、大理院正卿、法部侍郎、管理京师法律学堂事务大臣、资政院副总裁、袁世凯内阁司法大臣等职，并担任北京法学会会长。在此期间，他主持变法修律，为中国法律近代化做了奠基性工作。沈家本在法律改革中，以儒家的仁政和西方的人道主义为思想核心，以"法理"为中西法律的融会点，对旧律进行大刀阔斧改造的同时有选择地引进西方法律制度，倾注一生努力实现其以法治国、以法强国的理想。[1]

课 文

沈家本认为，历代法制和皇权统治莫不从"仁"字着墨，以"仁"为衡。"仁政"是儒家文化的重要政治内涵。孔子纳"仁"入"礼"，秦汉以后，历代统治者又一步步"纳礼入律"，传统法制中的一系列宽刑、轻刑、省刑措施和思想家的"德化""教化"等，就是这种"仁政"学说的具体表现。沈家本在继承儒家"仁政"思想以评判历代法制和指导清末修律的同时，也在一定程度上接受西方近代的"人道主义"思想，力主博采西法以补中法，使新法适应时局发展之需要。

沈家本在法律改革中，将中西两种异质法律的融会点选在"法理"上。"法理"一词，大约在中国东汉时期即已出现，彼时基本与"法律"同义。而近代意义上的"法理"概念随西学东渐的历史进程传入中国。

---

〔1〕 参见朱勇主编：《中国法律史》，中国政法大学出版社 2021 年版，第 313~315 页。

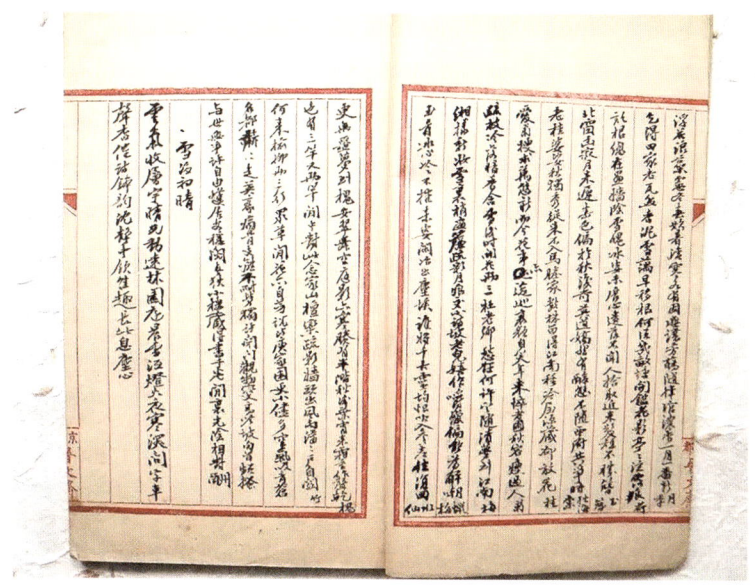

图 12-2　清·《枕碧楼偶存稿》[1]

　　"法理"一词，在清末较早见于沈家本的著作《刑案汇览三编》序中，此书中沈家本针对戊戌变法前后出现的新旧学说之争，发出如下议论："*顾或者曰：今日法理之学，日有新发明，穷变通久，气运将至，此编虽详备，陈迹耳，故纸耳。余谓：理固有日新之机，然新理者，学士之论说也。若人之情伪，五洲攸殊，有非学士之所能尽发其覆者。故就前人之成说而推阐之，就旧日之案情而比附之，大可与新学说互相发明，正不必为新学说家左袒也。*"在这里，他不但使用了"法理"概念，而且还对"新旧"（彼时多指中西）学说的相互关系、各自的长短做了初步论说。沈家本认为，中西法律法学都有各自的法理。双方法理尽管不完全相同，但总逃不出"情理"二字。用"情理"概括法理，并由此入手，贯通中西法学，正是沈家本的独到之处。《论杀死奸夫》是沈家本在修律过程中与礼教派相互辩难之作，他运用"法理"，就本夫有无权利杀死奸夫奸妇的问题进行了系统的论证。

―――――――

　　〔1〕转引自《纪念沈家本诞辰 180 周年 | 与沈家本有关的法制文物拾粹》，载"中国政法大学法律古籍整理研究所"公众号 2020 年 12 月 7 日，https://mp.weixin.qq.com/s/UXpZTHnfCyTVC8kvM-uBKw，最后访问日期：2025 年 5 月 30 日。

在沈家本的思想中，中外法律虽然各有自己的法理，但是，法理之大要——"情理"是相通的。融会贯通中外法学，就是要取中外法律中"合于情理"者，而舍其"悖于情理"者。"合于情理"者为善法、良法，"悖于情理"者为恶法、非法之法。[1]

 生词表

序号	生词	词性	汉语拼音	英文解释
1	法理	*n.*	fǎ lǐ	legal principle
2	着墨	*v.*	zhuó mò	elaborate on
3	内涵	*n.*	nèi hán	connotation
4	评判	*v.*	píng pàn	judge
5	时局	*n.*	shí jú	current political situation
6	异质	*adj.*	yì zhì	heterogeneous
7	西学东渐	*phr.*	xī xué dōng jiàn	the historical process of the diffusion of western academic thought into China from the late Ming Dynasty to modern times
8	论说	*n.*	lùn shuō	exposition and argumentation
9	情理	*n.*	qíng lǐ	common sense and human feelings
10	贯通	*v.*	guàn tōng	synthesize
11	独到之处	*phr.*	dú dào zhī chù	distinction or insight
12	辩难	*v.*	biàn nàn	retort with challenging questions
13	融会贯通	*idm.*	róng huì guàn tōng	gain a thorough understanding through integration
14	悖	*v.*	bèi	contrary to

重 点汉字【宰】

宰，汉语一级字。"宰"字始见于甲骨文，其字形上面是"宀"，表示房

---

[1] 参见朱勇主编：《中国法律史》，中国政法大学出版社 2021 年版，第 315~318 页。

屋；下面是"辛"，"辛"本义指刑刀——在屋里放置一把刑刀，表示被刺上记号的奴隶在屋里劳动，因此"宰"本义是"奴隶"，也可指奴隶主家中的奴隶总管，后引申为古代官吏的通称。在后世使用中，"宰"又被引申为屠宰、宰杀、割肉等义，在商业语境中，也比喻向顾客或服务对象索取高价，如"宰客"。

图12-3　"宰"字篆刻　（王琦 刻）

 汉字拓展

序号	词汇	汉语拼音	英文解释	例句
1	主宰	zhǔ zǎi	control,dominate	大自然主宰着万物的生长和变化。
2	宰相	zǎi xiàng	prime minister	宰相是中国封建时代对君主负责、总揽政务的最高官员。
3	宰杀	zǎi shā	slaughter	过年时，家家户户都会宰杀年猪，准备丰盛的年夜饭。
4	宰割	zǎi gē	invade，oppress and exploit	他不愿再像过去那样任由命运随意宰割。
5	宰客	zǎi kè	overcharge customers	听说那家酒店经常被人指责宰客。
6	宰制	zǎi zhì	dominate	在古代，皇权宰制着整个国家的政治走向。
7	宰相肚里能撑船	zǎi xiàng dù lǐ néng chēng chuán	be large-hearted	他待人宽容大度，从不计较个人得失，真是宰相肚里能撑船。

文 化知识【《历代刑法考》】

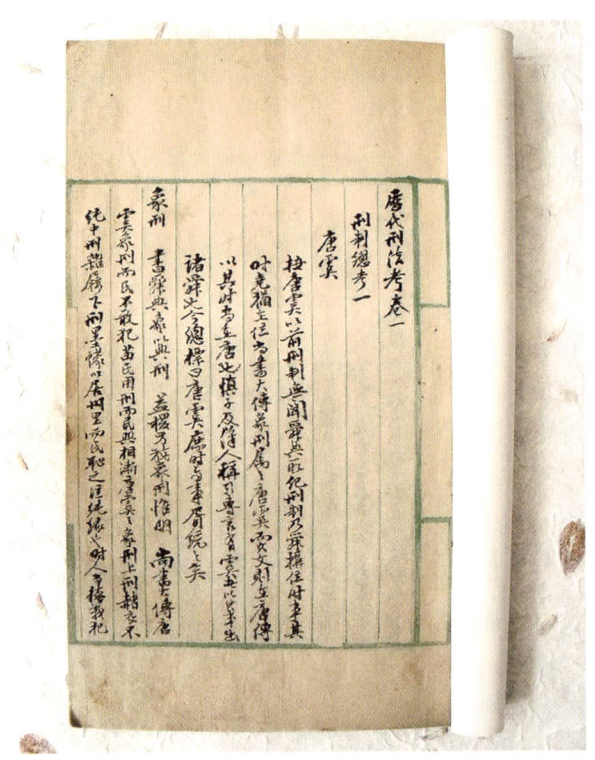

图 12-4　清·《历代刑法考》[1]

　　《历代刑法考》是沈家本的重要学术著作，该书对中国古代法律的源流、法律思想的变革、法典的发展变化、法学的兴衰以及历代法律的得失优劣进行了深入研究。《历代刑法考》七十八卷为《沈寄簃先生遗书》甲编的重要部分，包括《刑制总考》四卷、《刑法分考》十七卷、《赦考》十二卷、《律令》九卷、《明律目笺》三卷、《历代刑官考》二卷、《汉律摭遗》

---

　　〔1〕转引自《纪念沈家本诞辰 180 周年丨与沈家本有关的法制文物拾粹》，载"中国政法大学法律古籍整理研究所"公众号 2020 年 12 月 7 日，https://mp.weixin.qq.com/s/UXpZTHnfCyTVC8kvM-uBKw，最后访问日期：2025 年 5 月 30 日。

二十二卷，以及《狱考》《刑具考》《充军考》《明大诰峻令考》等经典内容，总计约150万字。该书上溯唐虞，下至明清，总考以五刑制度为基础，考察历代沿革；分考以具体刑罚为题，叙述各代的差异，为清末修律提供依据，推动了中国近代法律制度的改革发展，对研究中国法律制度的演变和发展具有不可替代的价值，让后人能更清晰地了解中国古代刑法的全貌和发展脉络，为现代法律制度的完善提供了历史借鉴和启示，是中国古代法律研究的必读之作。

法 治文物【沈家本著作木刻版】

图 12-5　沈家本著作木刻版[1]

现藏于中国政法大学图书馆的沈家本著作木刻版，由沈厚铎先生捐赠。沈家本著作木刻版为1913年前后由沈氏私家刊刻，目前整体保存良好，共计

---

〔1〕 参见《沈家本著作木刻版》，载中国政法大学中华法制文明虚拟博物馆，https://flgj.cupl.edu.cn/info/1072/3610.htm，最后访问日期：2024 年 12 月 10 日。

有《沈寄簃先生遗书》甲、乙编书版2842块，《枕碧楼丛书》1170块，《吴兴长桥沈氏家集》480块，总计4492板。内容除沈家本的经典著作如《历代刑法考》七十八卷外，还有诸多法律典籍旧钞本，如《宋刑统赋解》的四种钞本（昆陵董氏钞本《刑统赋解》，璜川吴氏钞本《粗解刑统赋》和《别本刑统赋解》，江阴缪氏钞本《刑统赋疏》)，以及绣谷吴氏旧钞本《内外服制通释》、朝鲜钞本《无冤录》等，对于古代法律及古代版本研究具有重要价值。

经 典阅读

《聊斋志异·促织》（节选）[1]

翼日进宰，宰见其小，怒呵成。成述其异，宰不信。试与他虫斗，虫尽靡。又试之鸡，果如成言。乃赏成，献诸抚军。抚军大悦，以金笼进上，细疏其能。既入宫中，举天下所贡蝴蝶、螳螂、油利挞、青丝额……一切异状遍试之，莫出其右者。每闻琴瑟之声，则应节而舞。益奇之。上大嘉悦，诏赐抚臣名马衣缎。抚军不忘所自，无何，宰以卓异闻。宰悦，免成役。又嘱学使俾入邑庠。后岁余，成子精神复旧，自言身化促织，轻捷善斗，今始苏耳。抚军亦厚赉成。不数年，田百顷，楼阁万椽，牛羊蹄躈各千计；一出门，裘马过世家焉。

异史氏曰："天子偶用一物，未必不过此已忘；而奉行者即为定例。加以官贪吏虐，民日贴妇卖儿，更无休止。故天子一跬步，皆关民命，不可忽也。独是成氏子以蠹贫，以促织富，裘马扬扬。当其为里正，受扑责时，岂意其至此哉！天将以酬长厚者，遂使抚臣、令尹，并受促织恩荫。闻之：一人飞升，仙及鸡犬。信夫！"

---

[1]《聊斋志异》是清代蒲松龄所著的文言短篇小说集。"聊斋"是蒲松龄的书斋名，"志异"旨在说明自己所记录的事情都是奇闻异事。《聊斋志异》以浪漫主义创作手法，讲述了众多花妖狐魅、鬼怪仙人的奇异故事，情节离奇曲折，充满想象力。作者借这些故事批判社会黑暗，讽刺科举弊端，也歌颂爱情、友情与人性美好。该书语言简洁明快，富有文采，是中国古代文言小说的巅峰之作，对后世文学产生了深远影响，至今仍为人们所喜爱，具有极高的文学价值和艺术魅力。

 参考译文

　　The next day, Cheng Ming presented the cricket to the magistrate. Upon seeing its small size, the magistrate angrily rebuked Cheng Ming for being perfunctory in his duties. When Cheng Ming told the magistrate about the cricket's remarkable abilities, the magistrate did not believe him. So, the magistrate had the cricket fight with other crickets, and all of other crickets were defeated one after another. Then he made the cricket compete with a rooster, and it turned out to be exactly as Cheng Ming had said. Therefore, the magistrate rewarded Cheng Ming and presented the cricket to the governor. The governor was extremely delighted upon hearing the report from the magistrate. He put the cricket in a golden cage and presented it to the emperor, and in his memorial to the throne, he elaborated in detail on the cricket's extraordinary skills. After the cricket arrived at the imperial palace, the emperor had it compete one by one with various rare crickets and other insects such as butterflies, mantises, Youlida, Qingsi'e that were tributed from all over the country. None of them could defeat the little cricket. Moreover, whenever there was music played, the cricket would dance gracefully in tune with the rhythm of the qin and se (traditional Chinese musical instruments). People were increasingly amazed by it, and the emperor liked it even more. As a result, the emperor was overjoyed and issued an edict to reward the governor with brocade fabrics and fine horses. The governor did not forget his subordinate who had presented the cricket. Soon, the magistrate was reported to the imperial court for his outstanding achievements in governance. When the magistrate was pleased, he exempted Cheng Ming from his forced labor and instructed the education official to allow Cheng Ming to enter the county school as a student. After about a year, Cheng Ming's son recovered his mental state. He said he had transformed into a cricket, being agile and good at fighting, and that he had just woken up now. The governor also rewarded Cheng Ming handsomely later. Within a few years,

Cheng Ming owned more than a hundred hectares of fertile land, numerous pavilions and buildings, and thousands of cattle and sheep. Every time he went out, he rode a tall horse and wore a sable fur coat, looking even more affluent than the renowned aristocratic families.

Pu Songling said: "When the emperor casually took an interest in a certain item, it was quite possible that he would forget about it soon after. However, the officials who were in charge of implementing related matters regarded it as a fixed rule. Moreover, with the officials being greedy and tyrannical, the common people had to pawn their wives and sell their children day by day, and there seemed to be no end to their suffering. Therefore, every move of the emperor was closely related to the lives and deaths of the common people, and it should never be overlooked! Only Cheng Ming was impoverished due to the extortion of corrupt officials. Later, he became wealthy because of presenting the cricket. In the end, he was riding on a well-fed horse and wearing a light fur coat, feeling extremely self-satisfied. When he was being punished as a village headman, how could he have ever imagined that he would end up like this? Heaven intended to reward the honest and kind-hearted people, so it made the governor and the magistrate also receive the rewards brought about by the cricket. As the old saying goes, 'When one person attains enlightenment, even his chickens and dogs rise to heaven.' It seems that this is indeed true!"

课 后练习

1.选择题：沈家本在清末法律改革中，将彼时中西两种异质法律的融会点选在（　　　）。

  A. 道理

  B. 情理

  C. 法理

  D. 事理

2. 判断题：近代意义上的"法理"大约在中国东汉时期出现。

3. 填空题：沈家本认为儒家文化的重要政治内涵是_____。

4. 简答题：说明沈家本融会中西法律的观点和独到之处。

5. 讨论题：从宽刑、轻刑、省刑措施以及"德化""教化"等角度，举例说明中国传统法中"仁政"的具体表现。

课 文参考翻译

Shen Jiaben believed that the legal systems and imperial rules throughout the dynasties all took the word "仁 benevolence" as the starting point and regarded "benevolence" as the criterion. "仁政 Benevolence governance" is an important political connotation of Confucian culture. Confucius incorporated "benevolence" into "礼 rites." After the Qin and Han Dynasties, successive rulers gradually "incorporated rites into laws." A series of measures such as lenient punishments, lighter punishments, and reduced punishments in traditional laws, as well as the concepts of "moral transformation" and "enlightenment" put forward by thinkers, are concrete manifestations of this doctrine of "benevolent government." While inheriting the Confucian idea of "benevolent governance" to evaluate the legal systems of past dynasties and guide the law revision in the late Qing Dynasty, Shen Jiaben also, to a certain extent, embraced the modern Western idea of "humanitarianism." He strongly advocated learning from Western laws to supplement Chinese laws, so as to make the new law adapt to the development needs of the current situation.

In the legal reform, Shen Jiaben chose "jurisprudence" as the point of integration of the two heterogeneous laws of China and the West. The term "jurisprudence" appeared in ancient China around the Eastern Han Dynasty and was basically synonymous with "law." The modern sense of the concept of "jurisprudence" entered China with the eastward progress of Western learning.

The term "jurisprudence" was first seen in the preface of Shen Jiaben's work *Compilation of Criminal Case Reviews III* in the late Qing Dynasty. In this book, in response to the controversy between the old and new doctrines that emerged before and after the Reform Movement of 1898, Shen Jiaben made the following remarks: "However, some people said, Today, the study of jurisprudence witnesses new inventions every day. As the principles of change and adaptation over time unfold, a new era is approaching. Although this compilation is comprehensive, it is but a thing of the past, just old records. I hold the view that there is indeed always an opportunity for new understandings of principles. However, these new principles are just the theories of scholars. Human deceptions and true natures vary greatly across the five continents, and there are aspects that even scholars are not capable of fully uncovering. Therefore, by expounding on the established theories of predecessors and making analogies based on past cases, it is highly possible to mutually illuminate and supplement new theories. There is really no need to show partiality towards the advocates of new theories." Here, he not only used the concept of "jurisprudence," but also made a preliminary discussion on the interrelationship and respective advantages and disadvantages of the old and new doctrines (at that time, it mostly referred to Chinese and Western doctrines). Shen Jiaben believed that both Chinese and Western legal theories have their own jurisprudence. Although the jurisprudence of the two sides is not exactly the same, it always boils down to the words "qingli" (common sense and human feelings). Generalizing jurisprudence with "qingli" and starting from this to bridge Chinese and Western jurisprudence is exactly Shen Jiaben's unique contribution. "On Killing an Adulterer" is a work in which Shen Jiaben debated with the ritualists during the process of law revision. He applied "jurisprudence" to systematically demonstrate the issue of whether the husband has the right to kill the adulterer and the adulteress.

In Shen Jiaben's thought, although Chinese and foreign laws each have their own jurisprudence, the essence of jurisprudence— "qingli" is universal. To integrate Chinese and foreign jurisprudence means to adopt the elements in Chinese and foreign laws that conform to "qingli" and discard those that are contrary to it. Laws that conform to "qingli" are regarded as good laws and sound legislation, while those that go against "qingli" are considered bad laws and unjust laws.

索引一

课文生词表汇总

序号	生词	词性	汉语拼音	英文解释	所在课文
1	案犯	*n.*	àn fàn	criminal	11
2	案件	*n.*	àn jiàn	case	11
3	白契	*n.*	bái qì	another term for "白契"	3
4	颁示	*v.*	bān shì	promulgate，announce	7
5	颁行	*v.*	bān xíng	promulgate	9
6	悖	*v.*	bèi	contrary to	12
7	变乱	*v.*	biàn luàn	alter and disrupt	7
8	辩难	*v.*	biàn nàn	retort with challenging questions	12
9	编纂	*v.*	biān zuǎn	compile，edit	5
10	并存	*v.*	bìng cún	coexist	5
11	驳正	*v.*	bó zhèng	refute and correct	8
12	不动产	*n.*	bù dòng chǎn	real estate，immovable property	3
13	草创	*v.*	cǎo chuàng	initiate，start from scratch	7
14	草契	*n.*	cǎo qì	informal or unofficial deed	3
15	漕运	*n.*	cáo yùn	grain transport by water	1
16	差遣制度	*n.*	chāi qiǎn zhì dù	a dispatch system where official titles were seperated from actual duties	2
17	猖獗	*adj.*	chāng jué	rampant，uncontrolled	4
18	朝觐	*v.*	cháo jìn	have an audience with an emperor	8
19	惩贪	*phr.*	chéng tān	punish corruption	9
20	成文法	*n.*	chéng wén fǎ	statutory law	5
21	赤契	*n.*	chì qì	another term for "红契"	3
22	重熙条制	*proper n.*	Chóng xī Tiáo zhì	the regulations promulgated during the Chongxi period of Emperor Xingzong of the Liao Dynasty	5

续表

序号	生词	词性	汉语拼音	英文解释	所在课文
23	刺面	v.	cì miàn	tattoo the face as a punishment	6
24	大理寺	n.	dà lǐ sì	the supreme court of the Ming Dynasty	8
25	大义	n.	dà yì	(in this article it refers to) the legal provisions	2
26	代称	n.	dài chēng	another name	10
27	档案	n.	dàng àn	archives	8
28	党派	n.	dǎng pài	political faction, party	1
29	帝师	n.	dì shī	the highest-ranking official in the Yuan Dynasty in charge of handing affairs related to Xizang and Buddhism	6
30	抵牾	v.	dǐ wǔ	conflict with	10
31	奠定	v.	diàn dìng	establish	8
32	动产	n.	dòng chǎn	personal property, movable property	3
33	都察院	n.	dū chá yuàn	the censorate in the Ming Dynasty	8
34	独到之处	phr.	dú dào zhī chù	distinction or insight	12
35	断案	v.	duàn àn	adjudicate, make a judgment	2
36	额	n.	é	forehead	4
37	耳目	n.	ěr mù	one who spies for somebody else	8
38	法定刑	n.	fǎ dìng xíng	statutory punishment	9
39	法规	n.	fǎ guī	laws and regulations	10
40	法理	n.	fǎ lǐ	legal principle	12
41	法律思想	phr.	fǎ lǜ sī xiǎng	legal thought	5
42	法律素养	n.	fǎ lǜ sù yǎng	legal literacy	2

续表

序号	生词	词性	汉语拼音	英文解释	所在课文
43	法制传统	*phr.*	fǎ zhì chuán tǒng	legal tradition	5
44	斐然	*adj.*	fěi rán	brilliant	10
45	分割	*v.*	fēn gē	divide，partition	2
46	风纪	*n.*	fēng jì	conduct and discipline	8
47	封建化	*n.*	fēng jiàn huà	feudalization	5
48	奉旨	*adv.*	fèng zhǐ	be at the emperor's order	11
49	富国强兵	*idm.*	fù guó qiáng bīng	enrich the country and strengthen the military	1
50	复核	*v.*	fù hé	review	11
51	复业	*v.*	fù yè	resume one's occupation or business	3
52	概不	*phr.*	gài bù	in no case	6
53	告发	*v.*	gào fā	report an offender，expose	4
54	更定	*v.*	gēng dìng	revise，amend	7
55	公章	*n.*	gōng zhāng	official seal	3
56	官吏	*n.*	guān lì	officials	2
57	贯通	*v.*	guàn tōng	synthesize	12
58	管辖	*v.*	guǎn xiá	govern，administer	6
59	广义	*n.*	guǎng yì	broad sense	10
60	规避	*v.*	guī bì	evade，avoid	3
61	国家机关	*phr.*	guó jiā jī guān	state organ	10
62	汉文化	*proper n.*	Hàn wén huà	Han culture	5
63	豪强	*n.*	háo qiáng	local tyrant，bully	7
64	红契	*n.*	hóng qì	red deed（officially stamped deed）	3
65	划定	*v.*	huà dìng	delimit，define	4

续表

序号	生词	词性	汉语拼音	英文解释	所在课文
66	皇统制	*proper n.*	Huáng tǒng Zhì	the statutory law promulgated during the reign of Emperor Xizong of the Jin Dynasty	5
67	饥民	*n.*	jī mín	famine victims	4
68	兼并	*v.*	jiān bìng	annex，merge	1
69	奸党	*n.*	jiān dǎng	treacherous cliques	9
70	监候	*n.*	jiān hòu	awaiting execution under surveillance	11
71	监禁	*v.*	jiān jìn	imprison	6
72	减免税赋	*phr.*	jiǎn miǎn shuì fù	tax reduction or exemption	3
73	缴纳	*v.*	jiǎo nà	pay，hand over	3
74	绞刑	*n.*	jiǎo xíng	hanging（execution）	9
75	结党	*v.*	jié dǎng	form factions	9
76	进士及第	*phr.*	jìn shì jí dì	passing the imperial examination and attain the degree of Jinshi	2
77	纠察	*v.*	jiū chá	supervise and rectify	8
78	均田制	*n.*	jūn tián zhì	equal-land system	3
79	拷掠	*v.*	kǎo lüè	torture	6
80	科举	*n.*	kē jǔ	imperial examination	2
81	滥杀	*v.*	làn shā	kill indiscriminately	11
82	里长	*n.*	lǐ zhǎng	head of a group of households	8
83	凌迟	*n.*	líng chí	slow slicing，death by a thousand cuts	7
84	论说	*n.*	lùn shuō	exposition and argumentation	12
85	弥补	*v.*	mí bǔ	compensate，remedy	8
86	没收	*v.*	mò shōu	confiscate	4

续表

序号	生词	词性	汉语拼音	英文解释	所在课文
87	内阁	*n.*	nèi gé	imperial cabinet	8
88	内涵	*n.*	nèi hán	connotation	12
89	奴婢	*n.*	nú bì	slave，servant	3
90	排挤	*v.*	pái jǐ	squeeze out	1
91	判处	*v.*	pàn chǔ	sentence	11
92	判决	*n.*	pàn jué	pronounce judgement	11
93	批示	*v.*	pī shì	write comments or instructions	11
94	评判	*v.*	píng pàn	judge	12
95	契税	*n.*	qì shuì	deed tax	3
96	弃田	*n.*	qì tián	abandoned land	3
97	强盗	*n.*	qiáng dào	robber	9
98	窃盗	*n.*	qiè dào	theft	9
99	侵害	*v.*	qīn hài	infringe，harm	6
100	情理	*n.*	qíng lǐ	common sense and human feelings	12
101	庆历新政	*proper n.*	Qìng lì Xīn zhèng	a political reform implemented during the Qingli period of the Northern Song Dynasty	1
102	倾注	*v.*	qīng zhù	pour into，devote	7
103	去指	*n.*	qù zhǐ	amputation of fingers	7
104	冗兵	*n.*	rǒng bīng	redundant soldiers	1
105	冗费	*n.*	rǒng fèi	redundant expenses	1
106	冗官	*n.*	rǒng guān	redundant officials	1
107	融会贯通	*idm.*	róng huì guàn tōng	gain a thorough understanding through integration	12

续表

序号	生词	词性	汉语拼音	英文解释	所在课文
108	三法司	*proper n.*	Sān fǎ sī	the Ministry of Punishments, the Court of Judicial Review and the Censorate as the Three Judicial Departments in the Ming and Qing Dynasties	11
109	丧葬费	*n.*	sāng zàng fèi	funeral expenses	6
110	色目	*proper n.*	Sè mù	a general term in the Yuan Dynasty for various ethnic groups in the northwest and western regions excluding the Mongols	6
111	僧侣	*n.*	sēng lǚ	monk	6
112	擅杀	*v.*	shàn shā	kill without authorization	11
113	烧埋银	*n.*	shāo mái yín	funeral expenses that muderers pay to the families of the victims	6
114	审录	*v.*	shěn lù	examine and record	11
115	时局	*n.*	shí jú	current political situation	12
116	时势	*n.*	shí shì	the current situation	11
117	受贿	*v.*	shòu huì	accept bribes	9
118	疏漏	*n.*	shū lòu	careless omission	8
119	司马光	*proper n.*	Sī mǎ Guāng	a statesman in the Northern Song Dynasty	1
120	素服	*n.*	sù fú	white mourning clothes	11
121	弹劾	*v.*	tán hé	impeach	8
122	淘汰	*v.*	táo tài	eliminate	1
123	题本	*n.*	tí běn	memorial on autumn assize	11
124	挑筋	*n.*	tiāo jīn	tendon severing	7
125	铁枷	*n.*	tiě jiā	iron necklock	6
126	廷杖	*n.*	tíng zhàng	imperial beating	9

续表

序号	生词	词性	汉语拼音	英文解释	所在课文
127	土地所有权	*n.*	tǔ dì suǒ yǒu quán	land ownership	3
128	挽救	*v.*	wǎn jiù	save，rescue	1
129	窝藏	*v.*	wō cáng	harbor，conceal	4
130	物主权	*n.*	wù zhǔ quán	ownership of goods	3
131	习惯法	*n.*	xí guàn fǎ	customary law	5
132	熙宁变法	*proper n.*	Xī níng Biàn fǎ	a reform implemented during the Xining period of the Northern Song Dynasty	1
133	系统	*n.*	xì tǒng	system	6
134	西学东渐	*phr.*	xī xué dōng jiàn	the historical process of the diffusion of western academic thought into China from the late Ming Dynasty to modern times	12
135	细则	*n.*	xì zé	detailed rules and regulations	10
136	狭义	*n.*	xiá yì	narrow sense	10
137	宪纲	*n.*	xiàn gāng	legal framework	8
138	先河	*n.*	xiān hé	precedent	9
139	心腹之患	*idm.*	xīn fù zhī huàn	major internal trouble	4
140	新旧	*phr.*	xīn jiù	new and old	1
141	新垦荒田	*phr.*	xīn kěn huāng tián	newly reclaimed wasteland	3
142	刑部	*n.*	xíng bù	the official department in charge of criminal law and prison litigation affairs in China's feudal society	6
143	刑名	*n.*	xíng míng	criminal cases and legal matters	8

续表

序号	生词	词性	汉语拼音	英文解释	所在课文
144	刑事特别法	*proper n.*	Xíng shì Tè bié fǎ	special criminal law	4
145	行政体制	*n.*	xíng zhèng tǐ zhì	administrative system	2
146	续编	*v.*	xù biān	continue to compile, additional compilation	7
147	续纂	*v.*	xù zuǎn	continue to compilation	8
148	宣仁太后	*proper n.*	Xuān rén Tài hòu	Empress Dowager Xuanren, the mother of Emperor Shenzong of the Northern Song Dynasty	1
149	徇私废公	*idm.*	xùn sī fèi gōng	act in self-interest and neglect public duties	7
150	严惩	*v.*	yán chéng	punish severely	6
151	业主	*n.*	yè zhǔ	property owner	3
152	一贯	*adj.*	yí guàn	consistent, all along	4
153	移徙	*v.*	yí xǐ	move, relocate	3
154	异质	*adj.*	yì zhì	heterogeneous	12
155	因俗而治	*phr.*	yīn sú ér zhì	governance according to customs	5
156	有价证券	*n.*	yǒu jià zhèng quàn	securities	3
157	御制	*adj.*	yù zhì	made by the emperor	7
158	圆审	*n.*	yuán shěn	the judicial review system in the Ming Dynasty	8
159	越诉	*v.*	yuè sù	the act of appealing beyond the level of authority	8
160	斋戒	*v.*	zhāi jiè	fast	11
161	摘叙	*v.*	zhāi xù	excerpt and narrate	11

续表

序号	生词	词性	汉语拼音	英文解释	所在课文
162	占有	*v.*	zhàn yǒu	possess，occupy	3
163	昭示	*v.*	zhāo shì	*make clear to all*	11
164	整顿	*v.*	zhěng dùn	rectify，reorganize	1
165	整齐	*v.*	zhěng qí	systematize，regulate	7
166	征收	*v.*	zhēng shōu	levy	6
167	争讼	*n.*	zhēng sòng	litigation，lawsuit	3
168	制定	*v.*	zhì dìng	formulate，establish	7
169	职官任免	*phr.*	zhí guān rèn miǎn	appointment and dismissal of officials	2
170	制决	*n.*	zhì jué	the emperor's ruling by decree	8
171	职务犯罪	*phr.*	zhí wù fàn zuì	official misconduct	9
172	重法	*phr.*	zhòng fǎ	severe law	4
173	注官	*v.*	zhù guān	review the qualifications of officials and determine their ranks and positions based on their abilities and achievements	2
174	株连	*v.*	zhū lián	implicate，involve others in a criminal case	4
175	诸夷	*phr.*	zhū yí	a general term for other border ethnic groups or tribes outside the Khitan in Liao Dynasty documents	5
176	着墨	*v.*	zhuó mò	elaborate on	12
177	奏报	*v.*	zòu bào	memorialize the emperor	11
178	奏释	*phr.*	zòu shì	submit a memorial to the throne to request the release of	6
179	祖制	*n.*	zǔ zhì	ancestral system	7
180	族诛	*n.*	zú zhū	extermination of a family or clan for a crime	7

索引二

课前准备生词表汇总

序号	生词	词性	汉语拼音	英文解释	所在课文
1	巴林左旗	*proper n.*	Bā lín Zuǒ qí	a county-level administrative region	5
2	被迫	*v.*	bèi pò	be forced, be compelled	1
3	编敕	*v.*	biān chì	compile imperial orders	2
4	编例	*v.*	biān lì	compile examples	2
5	编纂	*v.*	biān zuǎn	compile	10
6	布政司	*n.*	bù zhèng sī	the bureau of provincial administration in the Ming Dynasty	8
7	厂卫	*n.*	chǎng wèi	eunuch spies and royal guards, the imperial espionage agencies of the Ming Dynasty	8
8	朝臣	*n.*	cháo chén	court councillor	9
9	陈桥兵变	*proper n.*	Chén qiáo Bīng biàn	the mutiny incident in which Zhao Kuangyin overthrew the Later Zhou Dynasty and established the Song Dynasty	1
10	承前启后 承先启后	*idm.*	chéng qián qǐ hòu chéng xiān qǐ hòu	carry on the past and usher in the future	12
11	承袭	*v.*	chéng xí	inherit, adopt	1
12	敕	*n.*	chì	imperial order	2
13	冲击	*n.*	chōng jī	impact	12
14	传世	*adj.*	chuán shì	be handed down from ancient times	10
15	春秋 大一统	*phr.*	chūn qiū dà yī tǒng	the idea of achieving overall unity in various aspects during the Spring and Autumn Period in ancient China	11
16	担保	*v.*	dān bǎo	guarantee，assure	3

续表

序号	生词	词性	汉语拼音	英文解释	所在课文
17	党羽	*n.*	dǎng yǔ	henchmen	8
18	党争	*n.*	dǎng zhēng	factional strife	9
19	盗贼四起	*idm.*	dào zéi sì qǐ	rampant thievery	9
20	典当	*v.*	diǎn dàng	pawn	3
21	凋敝	*adj.*	diāo bì	decayed，destitute	3
22	定鼎	*v.*	dìng dǐng	establish the capital	10
23	定都	*v.*	dìng dū	establish the capital	1
24	夺取	*v.*	duó qǔ	seize, capture	1
25	法制建设	*phr.*	fǎ zhì jiàn shè	legal system construction	9
26	方针	*n.*	fāng zhēn	guiding principle	10
27	纲纪	*n.*	gāng jì	principles and discipline	9
28	庚子国变	*proper n.*	Gēng zǐ Guó biàn	the crisis year of 1900 involving the Boxer uprising and the eight nation military invasion	12
29	关键	*adj.*	guān jiàn	crucial	12
30	观念	*n.*	guān niàn	concept	11
31	国防	*n.*	guó fáng	national defence	12
32	汉化	*n.*	hàn huà	Sinicization	5
33	合流	*v.*	hé liú	merge，integrate	8
34	忽必烈	*proper n.*	Hū bì liè	the founding emperor of the Yuan Dynasty	6
35	互相为用	*phr.*	hù xiāng wéi yòng	be mutually beneficial	9
36	会宁	*proper n.*	Huì níng	the early capital of the Jin Dynasty	5
37	缉捕	*v.*	jī bǔ	arrest	8
38	继承	*v.*	jì chéng	inherit	10

续表

序号	生词	词性	汉语拼音	英文解释	所在课文
39	继往开来	*idm.*	jì wǎng kāi lái	carry a cause forward and forge ahead into the future	12
40	简当	*adj.*	jiǎn dāng	simple and appropriate	7
41	奸宄	*n.*	jiān guǐ	evildoer，malefactor	4
42	教有枢要	*phr.*	jiào yǒu shū yào	education focussing on key essentials	9
43	阶级矛盾	*n.*	jiē jí máo dùn	class conflict	4
44	禁军	*n.*	jìn jūn	imperial guards	1
45	进取	*adj.*	jìn qǔ	enterprising	9
46	军事统治	*phr.*	jūn shì tǒng zhì	military rule	5
47	刊版	*v.*	kān bǎn	cut blocks for printing	2
48	宽政待民	*phr.*	kuān zhèng dài mín	lenient policy towards the populace	4
49	框架	*n.*	kuàng jià	framework	11
50	例	*n.*	lì	example，precedent	2
51	礼法	*n.*	lǐ fǎ	rites and laws	7
52	礼法结合	*phr.*	lǐ fǎ jié hé	integration of rites and laws	9
53	礼义	*n.*	lǐ yì	propriety and righteousness	9
54	礼治	*n.*	lǐ zhì	rule by ritual	9
55	立足	*v.*	lì zú	base oneself upon	10
56	列强	*n.*	liè qiáng	great powers	12
57	领域	*n.*	lǐng yù	field	12
58	论证	*v.*	lùn zhèng	expound and prove	11
59	媒介	*v.*	méi jiè	mediate	12
60	蒙古大汗	*phr.*	měng gǔ dà hán	the common lord of all Mongols	6
61	民族矛盾	*phr.*	mín zú máo dùn	national contradiction	5

续表

序号	生词	词性	汉语拼音	英文解释	所在课文
62	谋大逆	*n.*	móu dà nì	the plotting of great treason	7
63	谋反	*n.*	móu fǎn	the plotting of a rebellion	7
64	农民起义	*n.*	nóng mín qǐ yì	the uprising of peasants who have lost their land, generally reflecting the contradictions between the autocratic imperial court and the civil society	6
65	女真	*proper n.*	Nǚ zhēn	Jurchen, an ethnic minority in the northeastern region of ancient China	5
66	契丹	*proper n.*	Qì dān	Khitan, an ancient nomadic people in China	5
67	迁	*v.*	qiān	move, migrate	1
68	人命关天	*idm.*	rén mìng guān tiān	human life is a matter of heaven, as human life is of crucial importance	11
69	善政	*n.*	shàn zhèng	good governance	9
70	上京	*proper n.*	Shàng jīng	the capital of the Liao Dynasty	5
71	商品经济	*n.*	shāng pǐn jīng jì	market economy	3
72	尚书	*n.*	shàng shū	a high-ranking official	2
73	社会矛盾	*phr.*	shè huì máo dùn	social contradiction	9
74	慎重	*adj.*	shèn zhòng	prudent	11
75	时弊	*n.*	shí bì	current malpractices	7
76	首推	*v.*	shǒu tuī	recommend first	12
77	松散	*adj.*	sōng sǎn	loose	3
78	贪赃枉法	*idm.*	tān zāng wǎng fǎ	embezzlement and perversion of law	7
79	体系化	*adj.*	tǐ xì huà	systematic	11

续表

序号	生词	词性	汉语拼音	英文解释	所在课文
80	提刑按察使	*n.*	tí xíng àn chá shǐ	a judge of the Provincial Surveillance Commission	8
81	天人合一	*idm.*	tiān rén hé yī	the unity of heaven and man, as human beings are an integral part of nature	11
82	铁木真	*proper n.*	Tiě mù zhēn	an outstanding strategist and statesman in world history	6
83	统领	*v.*	tǒng lǐng	command	8
84	挽狂澜于既倒	*idm.*	wǎn kuáng lán yú jì dǎo	save a dire situation	9
85	完颜阿骨打	*proper n.*	Wán yán Ā gǔ dǎ	the founding emperor of the Jin Dynasty	5
86	卫所	*n.*	wèi suǒ	military garrison and station	8
87	戊戌维新	*proper n.*	Wù xū Wéi xīn	the bourgeois reform movement in the late Qing Dynasty	12
88	相权	*n.*	xiàng quán	the power of the prime minister	8
89	享祚	*v.*	xiǎng zuò	reign over the throne	10
90	萧条	*adj.*	xiāo tiáo	depressed, sluggish	3
91	行为能力	*phr.*	xíng wéi néng lì	capacity for conduct, behavioral competence	3
92	修律	*v.*	xiū lǜ	revise laws	2
93	训诲	*v.*	xùn huì	instruct	11
94	逊位	*v.*	xùn wèi	abdicate	10
95	鸦片战争	*proper n.*	Yā piàn Zhàn zhēng	the war of aggression against China lunched by Britain	12
96	严惩不贷	*idm.*	yán chéng bù dài	punish severely without leniency	4
97	严典	*n.*	yán diǎn	strict rules	7
98	沿袭	*v.*	yán xí	inherit	8

续表

序号	生词	词性	汉语拼音	英文解释	所在课文
99	洋溢	*v.*	yáng yì	brim，overflow	9
100	耶律阿保机	*proper n.*	Yē lù Ā bǎo jī	the founding emperor of the Liao Dynasty	5
101	依附关系	*phr.*	yī fù guān xì	dependency relationship	3
102	依据	*n.*	yī jù	basis	11
103	易晓	*adj.*	yì xiǎo	easy to understand	7
104	印行	*v.*	yìn xíng	print and punish	2
105	由盛转衰	*phr.*	yón shèng zhuǎn shuāi	from prosperity to decline	9
106	云	*v.*	yún	say，express	11
107	酝酿	*v.*	yùn niàng	be in the making	10
108	杂居	*v.*	zá jū	reside in a mixed settlement, live together	5
109	灾祸	*n.*	zāi huò	disaster	11
110	责罚	*v.*	zé fá	punish	11
111	贼盗	*n.*	zéi dào	theft, robbery	4
112	招致	*v.*	zhāo zhì	bring about	11
113	正直	*adj.*	zhèng zhí	upright，honest	9
114	致良知	*phr.*	zhì liáng zhī	realize one's innate conscience	9
115	职掌	*v.*	zhí zhǎng	charge	8
116	重典	*n.*	zhòng diǎn	harsh legal measures	7
117	中都	*proper n.*	Zhōng dū	the capital of the Jin Dynasty	5
118	重绳	*v.*	zhòng shéng	severely punish	7
119	转型	*v.*	zhuǎn xíng	transform	12
120	纵弛	*v.*	zòng chí	be lax and indulgent in governing	7
121	租佃制度	*n.*	zū diàn zhì dù	tenancy system	3